OKS

199 Tax Deductions - E\ y ....ng the Taxman Doesn't Want You to Know About

THE COMPLEMENTARY WEBSITE

The http://books.indicator.co.uk website gives you instant access to all the ready-to-use documents, tools, policies, etc. that complement this publication.·

Go to

http://books.indicator.co.uk

and enter your access code
DXW749

THE CD-ROM

Don't have access to the Internet?
Call Customer Services on 01233 653500 to request a CD-ROM.

Indicator ☐ FL Memo

Indicator has joined forces with **FL Memo**

Cover: ©iStockphoto.com

First Edition - Second Print - E01P2

ISBN 978-1-906892-68-5

Introduction

This book shows you how to make the most of:

- *deductions from business profits*
- *deductions from an individual's income from an employment or directorship*
- *available input VAT deductions; and*
- *reliefs from Capital Gains Tax.*

The deductions from businesses apply, unless stated otherwise, to both unincorporated businesses and those operated through companies, and to both trading and property businesses.

For employments and directorships, many of the items concerned are taxable as income (if reimbursed by the employer - which is a necessity in some cases) but with a deduction or exemption available, so that no liability arises. In these cases, it will usually be possible for the employer to obtain a dispensation from the Taxman so that no reporting of the taxable amount will be necessary.

The input VAT deductions assume the context of a VAT-registered business that doesn't make any exempt supplies. If there isn't a VAT-registered business (and businesses that only make exempt supplies aren't able to register) the VAT won't be recoverable, and for businesses that make some exempt supplies the extent of the input VAT recovery might be limited.

We're always keen to receive feedback so if you have ideas for additional deductions please get in touch - we'll do our best to incorporate them in subsequent editions.

Stephen Kesby FCA CTA AIIT

Table of contents

Chapter 1   Land and buildings - capital expenditure

Chapter 2   Land and buildings - property rental and business use

Chapter 3   Motor vehicles

Chapter 4   Machinery, tools and equipment

Chapter 5   Goodwill, intellectual property,
software and websites

Chapter 6   Research and development

Chapter 7   Bad debts, losses and other accounting adjustments

Chapter 8   Travel, accommodation and subsistence

Chapter 9   Training, conferences and seminars

Chapter 10   Entertaining

Chapter 11 Advertising, promotion, gifts, samples and sponsorship

Chapter 12 Fines, penalties, damages and compensation payments

Chapter 13 Clothing, medical expenses and professional fees

Chapter 14   Publications and subscriptions

Chapter 15   Staff costs, pensions and employee share arrangements

Chapter 16   Finance costs and insurance

Chapter 17   Provision of finance

Chapter 18   Starting up in business

Chapter 19   Losses

Table of contents

Chapter 20 And finally...

Chapter 21 Documents

CHAPTER 1

Land and buildings - capital expenditure

Expenditure on acquiring, improving or altering land and buildings will generally be capital in nature, meaning that it can't be deducted. There are, however, a number of specific types of expenditure where relief can be obtained.

Deduction 1. Plant and machinery capital allowances

To the extent that it's attributable to any machinery or equipment, capital allowances can be claimed on expenditure on a building.

Additionally, where any works are carried out to a building in order to install machinery or equipment, the expenditure will also qualify for capital allowances.

Deduction 2. Capital allowances for fixtures

Where a building is purchased, to the extent that the purchase price can be attributed to fixtures in the building, capital allowances will also be available on those fixtures. Expenditure on fixtures other than integral features can be included in the main (18%) pool.

In order for this to be achieved, however, it will be necessary for the vendor and purchaser to make a joint election attributing the amount of purchase price that's attributable to the fixtures. With effect from April 2014 it will also be a requirement that the vendor was actually claiming capital allowances on the fixtures prior to sale.

This will apply not only to trading businesses, but also to property rental businesses. However, where the property concerned is residential and isn't a furnished holiday letting, capital allowances are only available in respect of items in any common parts of the property.

A furnished holiday letting is a commercial letting of furnished residential premises with a view to profit, that's broadly available for letting for at least 210 days in a tax year and which is actually let to members of the public for 105 days in the year. There are some other conditions and the 105 let days requirement is relaxed in certain circumstances.

Download Zone

For a **Capital Allowances Checklist and Capital Allowances Election**, visit **http://books.indicator.co.uk**. You'll find the access code on page 2 of this book.

Deduction 3. Capital allowances for integral features

As a subset of fixtures, special attention needs to be paid to expenditure on the acquisition and repair/replacement of integral features. Expenditure on integral features must be included in the special rate (8%) pool.

Additionally, repair expenditure on integral features will need to be treated as capital expenditure if either:

- it exceeds 50% of the replacement cost of the integral feature concerned; or
- taken together with other expenditure on the integral feature in the preceding twelve months, the total expenditure on the integral feature exceeds 50% of its replacement cost.

The integral features in a building are:

- electrical and lighting systems
- cold water systems
- space or water heating systems
- powered systems of ventilation, air cooling or air purification
- floors and ceilings comprised in the above two items
- lifts, escalators and moving walkways; and
- external solar shading.

Deduction 4. Buildings for research and development

Where a building is purchased for use for qualifying research and development, it will be eligible for research and development capital allowances.

Deduction 5. Business premises renovation allowances

Business premises renovation allowances are available for expenditure incurred on the conversion of commercial premises to qualifying business premises or the renovation or repair of qualifying business premises.

Qualifying business premises are unused buildings or structures located in a number of identified disadvantaged areas around the UK, and that will be used or let to be used for the purposes of a trade, profession or vocation, although certain trades are excluded.

A 100% initial allowance is available and to the extent that it isn't claimed, 25% allowances are available on the unclaimed balance, calculated on a straight line basis.

Deduction 6. Mineral extraction allowances

Mineral extraction allowances are available in respect of the acquisition of mineral deposits and rights. They are given on a reducing balance basis at 10% for expenditure on the acquisition of a mineral asset and 25% for other qualifying expenditure.

Deduction 7. Dredging allowances

Allowances are available in respect of capital expenditure on dredging and are given at 4% on a straight line basis.

Deduction 8. Rollover relief (full reinvestment)

Where certain assets (used for trade purposes) are sold (including land and buildings), giving rise to a chargeable gain, there is a relief available to reduce the amount of the taxable gain to the extent that the sale proceeds concerned are reinvested in replacement assets (also used for trade purposes).

Reinvestment in the replacement assets needs to occur within the period beginning one year before, and ending three years after, the sale of the old asset.

There are various categories of asset that qualify for rollover relief and the old and replacement assets don't necessarily need to be in the same category. The most notable categories of asset that qualify for rollover relief are:

- land and buildings
- goodwill
- fixed plant and machinery (which doesn't form part of a building or structure)
- ships, aircraft and hovercraft.

EXAMPLE

Prunaprismia Ltd has sold some trading premises (on April 30 2012) for £500,000, realising a chargeable gain of £300,000. If at some time in the period May 1 2011 to April 30 2015 it reinvests in a qualifying replacement asset, it can claim rollover relief to avoid the gain being immediately taxed.

It spends £600,000 acquiring new trading premises in May 2013, meaning that rollover relief can be claimed in respect of the gain on the old premises. Because the amount reinvested is more than the sale proceeds from the disposal of the old premises, the whole £300,000 gain can be rolled over.

The base cost of the new premises for chargeable gains purposes will be £300,000 (£600,000 cost less £300,000 rolled over gain).

Download Zone

For a **Rollover Relief Claim**, visit **http://books.indicator.co.uk**. You'll find the access code on page 2 of this book.

Deduction 9. Rollover relief (partial reinvestment)

To the extent that the sale proceeds aren't fully reinvested in new assets on a rollover, relief may still be obtained. The amount of chargeable gain that will remain taxable is the amount of sale proceeds that weren't reinvested.

EXAMPLE

If, in the previous example, Prunaprismia's new premises had only cost £400,000, £100,000 of the £500,000 proceeds from the sale of the old premises will not have been reinvested.

This means that £100 000 of the gain will have to remain chargeable (£200,000, therefore, having been rolled over).

The base cost of the new premises for chargeable gains purposes will be £200,000 (£400,000 cost, less £200,000 rolled over gain).

Deduction 10. Rollover relief (wasting assets)

If the asset into which the proceeds are reinvested is a wasting asset (with a useful life of less than 50 years), rollover relief only provides a temporary deferral; the rolled over gain will be charged to tax on the earliest of:

- ten years from acquisition of the replacement asset

- ceasing to use the asset for trade purposes; or

- a subsequent sale of the replacement asset (when rollover relief may again be available).

This will typically only apply in the case of land and buildings, where only a short (less than 50 years) leasehold interest is obtained.

EXAMPLE

If in the last example the replacement premises had been acquired under a short leasehold, then Prunaprismia would be charged to tax on the £200,000 rolled over gain once ten years had elapsed from acquisition. That is unless, in the meantime, it sold the interest replacement premises or ceased to use them for trade purposes, bringing the rolled over gain into charge sooner.

Deduction 11. Lease premiums - property businesses

Usually when a lease is granted for a premium it's a capital receipt chargeable to Capital Gains Tax (CGT) for the landlord and a capital expense for the tenant. This is deductible (in part in some circumstances) for CGT purposes from any proceeds or premium received on assignment of the lease or grant of a sub-lease.

However, where a landlord grants a short lease of 50 years or less, part of the premium will be charged to income tax as part of their property business profits.

The amount subject to income tax is 2% of the amount of the premium for each year by which the lease term falls short of a 51-year lease. For a one-year lease all of the premium will be chargeable to income tax and for a 50-year lease only 2% of the premium will be chargeable to income tax.

EXAMPLE

Robert is granting a ten-year lease to Andrew under which Andrew must pay a premium of £12,500. The lease falls 41 years short of 51 years, so Robert will have 82% (2% x 41) of the premium (£10,250) treated as part of his property business profits.

Where the tenant under such an arrangement is the proprietor of a property business, and charges a premium on a sub-lease of the premises, a proportion of the amount (relating to the sub-let period) that was taxed as income on the superior landlord, will be deductible from the amount taxable as income on them.

EXAMPLE

Andrew, from the above example, runs a property business and goes on to grant a five-year sub-lease to James for a premium of £6,500. This falls 46 years short of 51 years and so 92% (2 x 46) of the £6,500 premium (£5,980) is taxable on Andrew as income.

However, he can deduct from this £5,125 (£10,250 x 5/10ths) of the amount that was taxed as income on Robert. Andrew is, therefore, liable to income tax on £855.

Andrew would otherwise not have obtained any income tax deduction for the income element of the premium that he paid.

Deduction 12. Lease premiums - trading businesses

Where a trading business pays a premium on the granting of a short lease, the amount that is chargeable to income tax on the landlord can be spread over the term of the lease and taken as a deduction from the trade profits.

EXAMPLE

If instead of being the proprietor of a property business in the above examples, Andrew had taken the lease over premises for use in a trade, then for each year of the trade, he would be entitled to a tax deduction of £1,025 (the £10,250 taxable on Robert divided by the ten-year lease term).

Deduction 13. Only or main residence relief

Where an individual sells a property that is their only or main residence, any gain that might otherwise be chargeable to CGT is relieved from charge.

EXAMPLE

Richard and Judy have recently sold their sole residence for £500,000. It cost them £200,000 when they bought it eight years ago. The property was jointly owned and was occupied by them as their sole residence throughout their period of ownership.

Richard and Judy each have a gain of £150,000, but this won't be chargeable to CGT as full principal private residence (PPR) relief is available.

Full PPR relief is available in the example, because the property had been occupied by Richard and Judy as their main residence throughout their period of ownership. Where a property is occupied as the main residence for only a part of the period of ownership, the gain will need to be apportioned. The gain attributable to the period of occupation as a main residence only will be exempt from CGT.

However, in making this apportionment, the last three years of ownership of the property are treated as if it were occupied as the main residence, provided that there was a period of actual occupation as the main residence at some point during the period of ownership.

There are also a number of other periods of absence during which a property will be treated as occupied as the main residence if it was actually so occupied both at some time before and after the absence.

Deduction 14. Only or main residence lettings relief

Additionally, where there has been a period of occupation as the main residence and there is also a period during which any part of the property has been let, there is a further relief available, which is the smallest of:

* £40,000 per spouse or civil partner
* the gain attributable to the letting that would otherwise be a chargeable gain; and
* the exempt part of the gain attributable to use as the main residence (including the last three years).

EXAMPLE

Basil and Sybil have recently sold a property that they have owned for ten years and which they occupied as their main residence for the first three years. The property was empty for a year and was then let for the subsequent five of the remaining six years.

It was then empty again for the year before sale. They have made a gain of £100,000. £60,000 (6/10ths) of the gain (three years actual main residence and last three years deemed) is covered by PPR relief.

The gain that will be covered by the lettings extension of PPR relief is the smallest of:

- £80,000 (2 x £40,000),
- 30,000 (for three of the five years let that don't fall within the last three exempt years)
- £60,000 (already exempt).

So, £90,000 (£60,000 + £30,000) is exempt and only £10,000 is chargeable to CGT.

CHAPTER 2

Land and buildings - property rental and business use

This chapter covers a number of specific deductions that are available in respect of the use or occupation of land or buildings.

Deduction 15. Repairs to premises

Expenditure on genuine repairs to a building will be deductible. Something done to a building will be a repair if it simply restores it to its former state without replacing it entirely. If the building is altered or improved in any way, it's likely to be regarded as non-allowable capital expenditure.

If any element of alteration is incidental to work that is in the nature of a repair, because it's perhaps simpler or more expedient to carry out remedial work that results in an alteration to the property, then the expenditure will remain allowable.

Where the purpose of any work is to alter the property for some particular purpose, it will be capital in nature and non-allowable. Similarly, if any degree of improvement is incidental, because modern materials or technologies have changed, for example, then the expenditure will still be allowable if the purpose is remedial.

The replacement of wooden single glazed windows with modern UPVC double-glazed windows, for example, will not be regarded as an improvement, provided that the replacement is as like for like as is possible given the changing technologies and legal requirements, etc.

Conversely, if genuine repair works are being carried out and older materials are sought at a greater expense than their modern counterparts, because the building is listed, for example, the whole expense will still be allowable.

Finally, relief won't be allowable for what has been labelled notional repairs; where expenditure on a repair that would have been necessary is avoided by carrying out a non-allowable alteration or improvement.

Deduction 16. Provisions for lease dilapidations

As described under Deduction 82 in Chapter 7, a provision made by a tenant, where they have an obligation under their lease to make good any dilapidations that occur during the lease, will be an allowable tax deduction for a business if it satisfies the requirements of the Financial Reporting Standard 12.

Most tenants in this position carry out periodic maintenance every few years, and at the end of each period are able to make a tax deductible provision towards the future repair work.

Deduction 17. Renewals of fixtures

Fixtures are considered to be part of a building, and their replacement will generally be seen to be a repair to the larger entirety of the building. Expenditure on the replacement of fixtures can, therefore, usually be claimed as a revenue deduction from taxable business profits, provided there isn't a significant amount of improvement.

For example, replacing a fitted kitchen, a bathroom suite or toilet sanitary ware will qualify for relief as a repair in this way.

Deduction 18. Repairs and renewals of fittings

For businesses other than property businesses that let residential property, plant and machinery capital allowances will be available in respect of the fittings within a building.

For property businesses that let residential property, other than furnished holiday lettings, plant and machinery capital allowances are only available in respect of items in any common parts of residential buildings.

For these businesses, the fittings in the building (including any white goods) are likely to be regarded as implements, utensils or articles, meaning that any expenditure on their repair or replacement will be deductible as expenditure on trade tools.

Deduction 19. Repairs and renewals of furniture

For residential properties that are let furnished, but which aren't furnished holiday lettings, and in respect of which capital allowances can't, therefore, be claimed, there is a similar provision to allow the repair and replacement of furniture to be deductible.

Relief can't, however, be obtained for repairs and renewals of furniture if a wear and tear allowance is claimed.

Deduction 20. Wear and tear allowance for furnished properties

As an alternative to claiming for repairs and replacements of furniture (per Deduction 19 above), property businesses can claim a wear and tear allowance in respect of any property that is let furnished, and which isn't a furnished holiday letting.

The wear and tear allowance is 10% of gross rents less any utility bills paid by the landlord that would normally be the tenant's responsibility.

Deduction 21. Rent

Any rent paid by a business that it occupies for the purposes of its trade (in the case of a trading business) or that it sub-lets (in the case of a property business) can be deducted in calculating the taxable profits of the business.

Deduction 22. Business rates

Similarly, the business rates of a trading business are deductible.

Deduction 23. Council Tax - let property

For property businesses that incur Council Tax, either on behalf of its tenants or in respect of empty properties, the Council Tax expenses will also be deductible.

Deduction 24. Employee's accommodation

The revenue costs of providing an employee with accommodation, such as rents, utilities and Council Tax will be deductible.

Deduction 25. Use of home for the purposes of an unincorporated business

Where a sole trader or partner in an unincorporated business uses their home as an office, they can deduct appropriate proportions of their household expenses, including utilities, telephone, broadband, repairs, insurance, Council Tax and rent or mortgage interest.

The expenses should be apportioned based on estimated usage for things like telephone and broadband, and on the number of rooms and time that they're used for other expenses.

EXAMPLE

Derek runs his self-employed management consultancy business from home. In the year-ended March 31 2013, his mortgage interest was £3,500; Council Tax, £1,500; buildings and contents insurance, £500; and electricity and gas charges totalled £2,000. He also paid a maintenance contract covering his central heating system, for £500 per year.

The business does not use a significant amount of water and so, in accordance, with the Taxman's guidance he isn't including water charges in his use of home as office calculation.

Derek uses one of the bedrooms in his house (which has two reception rooms and four bedrooms in total) as his office, for around six hours a day, six days a week on average.

The total household costs listed above are £8,000 and Derek uses his one room for 36 hours per week on average. In total there are six rooms (bathrooms, toilets, kitchens and hallways aren't counted) that are used for 168 (24 x 7) hours in a week.

So Derek can claim £1,714 (£8,000 x 36/168) of the household costs as a deduction from his taxable business profits.

During the year he has also incurred broadband and telephone costs (that he estimates are used 60% for business purposes) totalling £500. Derek can claim a deduction of £300 (£500 x 60%) of these costs.

Deduction 26. Use of home for the purposes of a company business

Where a company owner-manager maintains a home office or regularly uses their home as an office, they can either avail themselves of Deduction 27 or they can enter into a licence agreement with the company and charge it a rent.

The rent should be no more than a market rent for the office accommodation provided; the costs as calculated for an unincorporated business's use of home as office charge (as in Deduction 25) can be deducted to determine the taxable rental profit of the owner-manager.

EXAMPLE

If Derek, in the above example, had operated through a limited company and a market value rent for the office (including use of phone and broadband) had been £200 per month, he would have rental income from the company of £2,400 and could deduct the above costs totalling £2,014, leaving him with a taxable rental profit of £386.

Download Zone

For a **Licence Agreement and Provision of Home Telephone Policy**, visit **http://books.indicator.co.uk**. You'll find the access code on page 2 of this book.

Deduction 27. Homeworker payments

Where an employee regularly performs some of the duties of their employment at home under arrangements between them and the employer, the employer can reimburse them for the additional household expenses that they incur as a result of working at home.

Evidence will only be required to support such a claim if the amount claimed exceeds £4 per week (or £18 per month).

This may be more convenient than Deduction 26 to company owner-managers, but might not give as good a result.

The additional costs can't, however, include a proportion of any fixed costs (such as broadband or telephone line rental) as the Taxman will say that these would have been incurred in any event.

EXAMPLE

Using this basis, Derek, from the previous examples (if he'd operated through a limited company), could have been reimbursed £216 tax-free by his company without needing to substantiate the claim. If he could demonstrate that his additional expenses were greater than that, he could be reimbursed a greater amount tax-free.

He would not, however, be able to claim anything in respect of the fixed costs of the telephone or broadband, nor the other fixed costs, such as mortgage interest, Council Tax, insurance, the maintenance contract and electricity and gas standing charges.

Download Zone

For a **Homeworkers' Expenses Policy**, visit **http://books.indicator.co.uk**. You'll find the access code on page 2 of this book.

Deduction 28. Rent-a-room relief

If someone obtains letting income from their main residence, or even trading income that's attributable to the letting of accommodation in the main residence, like receipts from a bed and breakfast business, it's possible to deduct deemed expenses of £4,250 in place of the actual business expenditure attributable to the letting (or trading) activity.

This will obviously only be worthwhile if the actual expenditure is less than £4,250 and a loss can only be created using the actual expenditure figure.

NOTE. Rent-a-room relief is only available in respect of the letting of accommodation and not where the space is going to be used as an office.

Download Zone

For an **Election for Rent-a-Room Relief Not to Apply**, visit **http://books. indicator.co.uk**. You'll find the access code on page 2 of this book.

CHAPTER 3

Motor vehicles

Expenditure relating to motor vehicles will often be capital in nature, so it can't be deducted from business profits for tax purposes. This chapter looks at how relief can be obtained for expenditure related to motor vehicles for businesses, as well as directors and employees.

Deduction 29. Capital allowances for motor vehicles

When a motor vehicle is first purchased the expenditure will qualify for capital allowances like any other machinery or equipment.

There are some restrictions that apply to cars though; the annual investment allowance can't be claimed in respect of expenditure on cars and short-life asset elections can't be made for cars.

Additionally, for cars that aren't eligible for a first year allowance, they will have to be included in the special rate (8%) pool, rather than the main (18%) rate pool if their CO_2 emissions exceed 130g/km.

Deduction 30. First year allowances for motor vehicles

Some motor vehicles will qualify for a 100% first year allowance. These are new goods vehicles with zero CO_2 emissions and new cars with CO_2 emissions of 95g/km or less.

Deduction 31. Car hire for employees and directors

If a director or employee needs to hire a car for the purposes of business travel necessary in their employment, the cost will be deductible from their taxable employment income.

Where the employer pays for such a cost, it's a taxable benefit, but the employee or director will have a corresponding expense to deduct from the taxable benefit.

Deduction 32. Car hire and leasing for businesses

The cost of hiring or leasing a car for business purposes will be a deductible expense. The amount that can be deducted is, however, restricted by 15% if the CO_2 emissions of the car exceed 130gm. This restriction will not apply to short term car hire of less than 45 days.

Deduction 33. Capital contributions towards company cars

Where someone is provided with a car by reason of their employment and it's available for their private use, there will be a benefit in kind, which will normally be a percentage of the manufacturer's list price.

For the purposes of this calculation any capital contribution (up to a maximum of £5,000) made by the employee towards the provision of the car can be deducted before applying the relevant percentage to calculate the benefit.

Deduction 34. Contributions towards private use of company vehicles

For cars provided by an employer that are available for private use, any contribution made by the employee or director for that private use will result in a £1 for £1 reduction in the benefit in kind.

The same applies for vans provided by an employer, where there is a fixed benefit of £3,000 if available for private use, as well as any other vehicles which give rise to a benefit in kind.

Deduction 35. Mileage allowance and relief for employees and directors

Where employees use their own vehicles for business purposes they can receive a tax and NI-free payment from their employers.

For cars and vans, the amount is 45p per mile for the first 10,000 miles and 25p per mile beyond 10,000 miles; for motorcycles, the amount is 24p per mile. There is also a rate of 20p for bicycles used for business journeys.

Where the employer doesn't pay these mileage allowances, the amounts can be claimed as an expense of the employment.

No other amounts, including capital allowances, can be claimed by an employee or director in respect of the use of their own vehicles for work purposes.

Deduction 36. Passenger payments for employees and directors

In addition to mileage allowances, an employer can pay an employee an amount of 5p per mile for each mile of a business journey where the employee or director has a passenger in their car or van. For each passenger who is an employee travelling for business the amount can be multiplied by each passenger.

Passenger payments aren't available for motorcycles or bicycles and, unlike mileage, the relief can't be claimed if the employer doesn't pay an allowance.

Deduction 37. Motor vehicle running costs for the self-employed

The self-employed can claim a proportion of all their costs of owning and running a vehicle to the extent that it's used for business purposes.

Relief will be obtained for the cost of the car by way of capital allowances.

Relief for any costs of financing the purchase, as well as running the vehicle can be deducted directly from the taxable business profits after applying an appropriate restriction for any private use of the vehicle.

> EXAMPLE
>
> David has a car that he uses both for his business and for his personal use. He estimates that his personal use of the car is 40%.
>
> During the year ended March 31 2013 his running costs of the car were: car tax - £130; insurance - £500; breakdown insurance - £270; servicing, maintenance and repairs - £600; car loan interest - £500; petrol - £2,000. He has travelled around 7,500 business miles in the year.
>
> He has spent a total of £4,000 of which 40% (£1,600) is attributable to private use and he can claim the other £2,400 as a deduction from his taxable business profits. His capital allowances claim will also be restricted by 40% for the private use.

Deduction 38. Mileage allowances for the self-employed

An alternative to claiming a proportion of the actual costs of owning and running a motor vehicle, that's available to unincorporated businesses, is to claim a deduction from taxable business profits using mileage rates.

If deductions are made on this basis no capital allowances can be claimed, however.

> EXAMPLE
>
> David, from the previous example, could have claimed £3,375 (7,500 x 45p) under this method, in place of his £2,400 expenses plus capital allowances.

Up until April 5 2013, this option was only available where the turnover of the business was below the VAT registration threshold at the time the vehicle was first used for business purposes.

It was also possible to claim any financing costs in addition to the mileage rate. This is no longer possible with effect from April 6 2013.

Deduction 39. Passenger deductions for the self-employed

Where mileage payments are used by an unincorporated business, a deduction could also be claimed for the years 2011/12 and 2012/13 for passengers. The amount was 5p per passenger, per business mile travelled.

Deduction 40. Input VAT recovery on motor vehicle purchases

Where a motor vehicle will have business use, the input VAT can be recovered on its purchase. This won't, however, be the case for a car unless it will be used exclusively for business purposes.

Where input VAT is recovered on the purchase of a vehicle that's also used for private purposes there will need to be an output VAT adjustment for each of the first five years following purchase, equivalent to the private proportion of 1/5th of the input VAT originally recovered.

Deduction 41. Input VAT recovery on motor vehicle leasing

Similarly, where the motor vehicle is leased, the input VAT on the lease payments can be fully recovered. For cars, only 50% of the input VAT can be recovered, unless it's used exclusively for business purposes.

Where the input VAT is fully recovered and there's private use of the vehicle, there will need to be a corresponding output VAT adjustment.

Deduction 42. Input VAT recovery on fuel

There are three ways of dealing with the recovery of input VAT on fuel, where there is also private use of the vehicle. Either:

*   no input VAT is recovered on any fuel; or
*   mileage records are kept and input VAT is only recovered on the business proportion; or
*   input VAT is recovered on all fuel.

In the latter case, mileage records will need to be kept and an output VAT adjustment made for the private use, which would be equivalent to the input VAT recovered on the private element. In the case of cars, this output VAT adjustment is replaced by a scale charge based on the CO_2 emissions.

Deduction 43. Input VAT recovery on other motor vehicle running costs

Where a motor vehicle is used for business purposes, input VAT can be fully recovered on all other running costs.

CHAPTER 4

Machinery, tools and equipment

Expenditure on machinery, tools and equipment (including computers) will generally be regarded as capital in nature, meaning that it can't be deducted in calculating the taxable profits of a business. This chapter looks at how tax relief can be obtained for this sort of expense for both businesses and employees/directors.

Deduction 44. Repairs to machinery, tools and equipment

Any necessary repairs to machinery tools and equipment will be deductible, provided that the asset concerned isn't significantly altered or improved.

Expenditure on alteration of an asset is generally regarded as capital expenditure, but remains specifically deductible provided no material new asset of significance results from the expenditure.

Deduction 45. Replacement of small tools

Similarly, there is a deduction expressly permitted for the replacement of trade tools, which includes any implement, utensil or article used for the purposes of the business. This will apply to tools and smaller items of equipment, but would not apply to large items of equipment or machinery.

Deduction 46. Capital allowances for companies

For expenditure on machinery, tools and equipment by companies, relief is given by way of plant and machinery capital allowances.

Subject to Deductions 50 and 51, expenditure on new plant and machinery is added to a pool of expenditure and any proceeds from disposals of assets (limited to the original cost of the assets concerned, where sale proceeds exceed original cost) is deducted from the pool. A writing down allowance is then deducted from the pool balance each year, calculated on a reducing balance basis.

There are two available pools of expenditure: the main pool, which includes most expenditure (particularly in relation to machinery, tools and equipment), and the special rate pool, which includes expenditure on cars and integral features. Writing down allowances on the main pool are at 18% and writing down allowances on the special rate pool are at 8%.

EXAMPLE

Mavramorn Ltd is calculating its capital allowances for the year ended March 31 2013. It has balances brought forward on its main pool and special rate pool of £30,000 each.

It has spent £20,000 in the year on machinery, which will be included in the main pool and it has sold an asset that cost £5,000 and was included in the special rate pool for £6,000.

It will calculate its capital allowances as follows:

	MAIN POOL (£)	SPECIAL RATE POOL (£)
Brought forward	30,000	30,000
Additions	20,000	-
Disposals (£6,000 but limited to cost)	-	(5,000)
	50,000	25,000
Writing down allowance (@18%/8%)	(9,000)	(2,000)
Carried forward	41,000	23,000

The total writing down allowances of £11,000 will be a deduction when the company goes on to calculate its taxable business profits.

Where the company's accounting period is less than twelve months, the writing down allowances will need to be pro rata of that figure.

Deduction 47. Capital allowances for unincorporated businesses

Plant and machinery capital allowances work exactly the same for unincorporated businesses as they do for companies, with two exceptions.

Firstly, unincorporated businesses are able to have basis periods that are longer than twelve months. In this case, writing down allowances are broken down pro rata to a maximum period of 18 months. If the basis period is longer than 18 months, it's broken into twelve months and residual periods for capital allowances purposes.

The second exception relates to assets that have private use, which are looked at in Deduction 55.

Deduction 48. Capital allowances for directors and employees

Where a director or employee spends money on assets that they use for the purposes of their employment, they too are able to claim plant and machinery capital allowances against their employment income, with the tax year as their basis period.

Any asset that also has private use will be dealt with as per Deduction 55.

Employees and directors can't, however, claim capital allowances on their own vehicles used for business purposes.

Deduction 49. Leasing assets to your company and claiming capital allowances

For company owner-managers, an alternative to claiming capital allowances against their employment income (which will also be liable to NI) is to own assets personally and lease them to the company.

The full range of deductions covered in this chapter will then be available, except first year allowances dealt with in Deduction 51. Short-life asset elections dealt with in Deduction 54 will also not be possible.

Deduction 50. The annual investment allowance

All expenditure for which plant and machinery allowances can be claimed will first be eligible for the annual investment allowance (AIA), which applies before expenditure is added to any pool.

The AIA is an amount of qualifying expenditure on which a 100% allowance can be claimed each period. Since January 1 2013 the annual amount of the allowance has been £250,000. It had previously been £25,000 and will revert to that amount on January 1 2015.

Periods that straddle these date will take the apportioned amount of each of the relevant allowances; periods of more or less than a year will also need to be worked out pro rata.

EXAMPLE

Coalblack Ltd has an eleven month period ended April 30 2013. Its maximum AIA is £97,917 (£25,000 x 7/12ths + £250,000 x 4/12ths). It will receive a 100% allowance on nominated expenditure up to that amount, which can be deducted in calculating its business profits.

The AIA is best used against expenditure that needs to be included in the special rate (8%) pool in priority to that which can be included in the main (18%) pool in order to maximise total capital allowances.

Deduction 51. First year allowances

Before any expenditure that qualifies for capital allowances is considered for inclusion within the AIA or added to any pool, it may be eligible for a 100% first year allowance.

There's no maximum first year allowance, it's determined by having expenditure of a qualifying type, and first year allowances do not need to be worked out pro rata for short periods.

The main types of expenditure that will be eligible for 100% first year allowances are:

- energy saving and environmentally beneficial plant and machinery

- new goods vehicles with zero CO_2 emissions new cars with low CO_2 emissions.

Certain plant and machinery to be used in designated areas within enterprise zones.

First year allowances can't be claimed on assets that are let on hire in any way and aren't available in the period of cessation of a business.

Deduction 52. Small pool write offs

Where the balance on a pool immediately before claiming a writing down allowance is £1,000 or less, the entire pool balance can be claimed as a writing down allowance.

EXAMPLE

Griffle Ltd has a balance brought forward on its main pool of £2,900 and has new expenditure to add to the pool of £2,000. It has sold an asset in the year (that originally cost £6,000) for £4,000.

It will calculate its capital allowances as follows:

	£
Balance brought forward	2,900
Additions	2,000
Disposals (proceeds less than original cost)	(4,000)
	900
Writing down allowance (pool balance £1,000 or less)	(900)
Balance carried forward	-

Deduction 53. Balancing adjustments

If at any time the amount to be deducted from the pool exceeds the pool balance, there will be a taxable balancing charge.

EXAMPLE

Drinian Ltd has a balance brought forward on its main pool of £8,000 and has sold an asset in the year (that originally cost £20,000) for £10,000.

It will calculate its capital allowances as follows:

	£
Balance brought forward	8,000
Disposals (proceeds less than original cost)	(10,000)
Balancing charge (taxable)	(2,000)

There is a corresponding deductible allowance, the balancing allowance, which is available when the proceeds received are less than the residual balance. This is only available, however, when the business permanently ceases or for the single asset pools described in Deductions 54 and 55.

Deduction 54. Short-life assets

To enable businesses to access the balancing allowance on assets that are expected to have a short useful life and which will be sold for less than their tax written down value, a short-life asset election is available. This election needs to be made on an asset-by-asset basis and has the effect of putting the asset in its own separate pool.

Writing down allowances will be given on this single asset pool at the rate that would have applied without the election. On disposal of the asset either a balancing charge or a balancing allowance will arise.

If the asset has not been disposed of by the eighth anniversary of the end of the period in which it was acquired, any residual balance will be transferred back to the appropriate pool at the beginning of the next period. This eight-year period was only four years where the acquisition expenditure occurred before April 2011.

EXAMPLE

Rabadash Ltd has an asset that it bought four years ago for £30,000 and in respect of which it made a short-life asset election. The asset would otherwise have been included in the main pool. The asset has been sold in the current period for £12,000 and its single asset pool has a balance brought forward of £16,000.

Rabadash will, therefore, have a balancing allowance of £4,000 in the current period.

If the asset hadn't been sold, Rabadash would have claimed a writing down allowance at 18% (£2,880) and the residual £13,120 would have been transferred to the main pool at the beginning of the next period.

Machinery, tools and equipment

4

A short-life asset election can't be made in respect of an asset that is let on hire and the small pool write-off described in Deduction 52 isn't available to single asset pools.

Download Zone

For a **Short-Life Asset Election** visit **http://books.indicator.co.uk**. You'll find the access code on page 2 of this book.

Deduction 55. Assets with private use in unincorporated businesses

For unincorporated businesses, any asset that has both business and private use must be kept in its own separate asset pool and the allowances calculated must be restricted in respect of the private use.

Writing down allowances (which will be restricted for private use) will be given at the rate that would have applied if the asset didn't need to be separately pooled. The residual expenditure on this separate asset pool will never stay in the single asset pool until the asset is disposed of, regardless of how long that may be.

On disposal a balancing allowance or charge will arise.

EXAMPLE

Simon bought a pie-making machine for £500 last year that he uses privately for 20% of the time. He sold the machine this year for £300.

Last year he would have calculated his capital allowances for the pie-machine as:

	£
Additions	500
Writing down allowance (18%)	(100)
Balance carried forward	(400)

He would have reduced the writing down allowance to £80 in respect of his 20% private use before aggregating it with his other capital allowances to deduct from his business profits.

This year he will calculate the capital allowances as:

	£
Balance brought forward	400
Disposals	(300)
Balancing allowance	100

The balancing allowance will again be restricted to £80 in respect of the 20% private use prior to being deducted from Simon's business profits.

Note. The small pool write-off isn't available for a single asset pool.

Deduction 56. Rollover relief for plant and machinery

Where assets qualifying for plant and machinery capital allowances are sold at a profit, in addition to the balancing charge that will arise, there will be a chargeable gain.

If the asset concerned is fixed plant and machinery and the proceeds of disposal have been, or will be, reinvested, it may be possible to claim rollover relief for the gain.

Deduction 57. Input VAT recovery

Input VAT will be recoverable on machinery, tools and equipment purchased for the purposes of the business.

If there's private use of any asset, an output VAT adjustment will need to be made over each of the first five years following acquisition equivalent to the private proportion of one fifth of the input VAT originally recovered.

Machinery, tools and equipment

4

CHAPTER 5

Goodwill, intellectual property, software and websites

Many businesses at some point purchase intangible assets, such as goodwill and other intellectual property. Often unincorporated businesses go on to incorporate and transfer goodwill and other intangibles to the company. Most businesses use software to some extent and most will maintain a website.

This chapter considers the various different ways that tax relief might be obtained for such expenditure.

Deduction 58. Corporate intangibles - amortisation

Where a company acquires goodwill or another intangible asset from an unconnected party or a connected party that itself acquired or created the asset after March 31 2002, it will be able to obtain a tax deduction for the debit entries in its accounts drawn up in accordance with accounting standards.

No deductions will, however, be permitted for any capitalised research and development (R&D) costs on which the R&D reliefs for revenue expenditure, looked at in Chapter 6, have been claimed.

Accounting standards require that intangible assets should be amortised to their estimated residual value over their estimated useful lives, and this writing off will be a tax deductible expense.

It should be noted, however, that, where a business incorporates, any goodwill transferred will only qualify for this treatment if the transferring (and by definition connected) business commenced after March 31 2002. Where the business was carried on before April 1 2002, all the goodwill is deemed to have been created before that date by the legislation.

EXAMPLE

Alan has recently incorporated his business (which he originally set up in 2003) and has sold his goodwill to his new company for its market value of £100,000. The expected useful life to the company of the acquired goodwill is four years, when there is not expected to be any residual value.

The goodwill is, therefore, amortised over the four years on a straight-line base: £25,000 per year.

Whilst Alan is connected to the company, because his previous unincorporated business commenced after March 31 2002, the company will obtain tax relief on the £25,000 per year writing off deductions.

Download Zone

For a **Calculation of Goodwill Pro Forma**, visit **http://books.indicator.co.uk**. You'll find the access code on page 2 of this book.

Deduction 59. Corporate intangibles - impairment

Similarly, if an intangible asset on which the amortisation is allowable needs to be impaired, because its value is now less than the amount at which it's shown in the company's balance sheet, the amount of the impairment will be tax deductible.

Obentinus Ltd purchased a brand name a few years ago that is now shown in its balance sheet at £20,000. Due to safety concerns over a similarly named product, the brand is now considered worthless and is being fully impaired.

The £20,000 impairment will be deductible in calculating the company's taxable profits.

Deduction 60. Corporate intangibles - losses on disposal

Where an intangible asset to which Deductions 58 and 59 apply is sold, any accounting loss arising on disposal will be deductible in calculating the taxable business profits.

Deduction 61. Corporate intangibles - rollover relief

Where such an intangible asset is sold and an accounting profit arises, that profit is taxable.

There is, however, a form of rollover relief for corporate intangibles. The proceeds from the sale of the old intangible asset will need to be reinvested in the purchase of a replacement intangible asset during a period starting one year before and ending three years after the disposal of the old intangible asset.

Deduction 62. Goodwill for unincorporated businesses

Any expenditure on goodwill acquired by an unincorporated business (or by an incorporated business to which Deductions 58 to 61 do not apply) can only be deducted in calculating the chargeable gain on a subsequent disposal of the goodwill by the business.

Deduction 63. Goodwill for unincorporated businesses - rollover relief

Where goodwill is sold by an unincorporated business (or by an incorporated business to which Deductions 58 to 61 do not apply), any gain arising may be eligible for rollover relief.

Goodwill, intellectual property, software and websites

5

Deduction 64. Know-how for unincorporated businesses

Where an unincorporated business acquires know-how, the expenditure will ultimately be deductible in calculating any chargeable gain on any future sale.

In the intervening period the expenditure will be eligible for know-how capital allowances, which are calculated on a pooled basis (as for plant and machinery capital allowances), with writing down allowances calculated at 25% on a reducing balance basis.

Know-how for this purpose is industrial information or techniques likely to assist in:

- the manufacture of goods or materials
- the working of a source of mineral deposits; or
- the carrying out of any agricultural, forestry or fishing operations.

Payments under franchise arrangements and things like market research, customer lists and sales techniques don't qualify as know-how.

Deduction 65. Patents for unincorporated businesses

Similarly, where an unincorporated business acquires patents, the expenditure will ultimately be deductible in calculating any chargeable gain on any future sale.

In the intervening period the expenditure will be eligible for patent capital allowances, which are again calculated on a pooled basis (as for plant and machinery capital allowances), with writing down allowances calculated at 25% on a reducing balance basis.

Deduction 66. Other intellectual property for unincorporated businesses

For any other intellectual property acquired by an unincorporated business, the expenditure will only be available as a deduction in calculating any future capital gains.

Deduction 67. Registration of patents and other intellectual property

Where any business is creating its own intellectual property which needs to be registered, as is the case for trademarks and patents, the cost of registration is allowable.

Goodwill, intellectual property, software and websites

Deduction 68. Computer software

Computer software purchased with a computer will qualify for capital allowances along with the computer.

The cost of computer software purchased separately can be deducted if its expected useful life is two years or less. Where the expected useful life is more than two years, capital allowances can be claimed.

Deduction 69. Website expenditure

Planning costs for a website are deductible in calculating a business's taxable profits, as generally will be the case for the development costs of the website.

The development costs should be treated as an asset and capital allowances claimed if the development costs relate to bringing into being an asset that will earn revenues, such as an online shop.

Domain names should be treated as intellectual property, dependent on whether the business is operated through a company or is unincorporated.

CHAPTER 6

Research and development

A number of specific tax reliefs/deductions aimed at businesses, which incur expenditure in relation to research and development (R&D), are examined in this chapter.

Deduction 70. Basic revenue relief for R&D expenditure

Both companies and unincorporated businesses can obtain a deduction for expenditure of a revenue nature on R&D, whether or not that expenditure is capitalised under accounting standards, provided it relates to the trade or intended trade and is directly undertaken by the person (i.e. it isn't sub-contracted).

Deduction 71. Enhanced revenue relief for R&D expenditure

Enhanced reliefs enable a company to take a Corporation Tax deduction in excess of the amount of expenditure actually incurred, and are broadly only available on expenditure for the company's own qualifying R&D (not R&D that is sub-contracted to the company), that is revenue in nature.

For SMEs, the rate of enhancement (for expenditure incurred on or after April 1 2012) is 125%, so that relief is given on 225% of the amount actually spent. That is a relief in terms of tax payable of between 45% and 55% of the amount spent, dependent on the company's tax rate.

> EXAMPLE
>
> Jadis Ltd has spent £50,000 on qualifying R&D expenditure in its year ended March 31 2013. This will be enhanced by 125% to £112,500, which will be deducted from the company's taxable profits, on which it would pay Corporation Tax at 20%.
>
> Jadis will therefore obtain Corporation Tax relief of £22,500 (£112,500 x 20%) on the enhanced expenditure, equivalent to 45% of the amount actually spent.

To be eligible for the SME reliefs, the company must be a going concern, the expenditure must not be subsidised (the qualifying expenditure will be reduced by the subsidy unless it constitutes state aid) and the total tax relief being obtained for any project must not exceed €7.5 million (the state aid cap).

For subsidised expenditure that constitutes state aid and for expenditure that breaches the state aid cap, as well as expenditure by an SME on R&D that has been sub-contracted to it by a large company, enhancement can be obtained at the large company rate (below).

For large companies, the rate of enhancement is 30%, meaning that the company obtains a deduction for 130% of the actual expenditure, giving relief in terms of tax of 31% of the amount spent.

A company will be an SME for this purpose if it (taken together with other companies in its group) has fewer than 500 employees and either has a turnover of no more than €100 million or total assets of no more than €86 million. A company that doesn't meet the criteria will be a large company.

Deduction 72. R&D tax credits

For an SME company, where a loss arises in the period, then to the extent that the loss can be taken to comprise enhanced R&D expenditure it can be surrendered (giving up the right to use the loss in some other way) in exchange for a tax credit repayable by the Taxman.

The amount of the repayable tax credit is 11% of the loss so surrendered, which gives an effective rate of tax on the underlying expenditure of 24.75%.

EXAMPLE

If instead of having a profit, Jadis, as in the previous example, had a loss of £100,000, the whole amount (being less than the £112,500 enhanced R&D expenditure) would be attributable to enhanced R&D expenditure and could be surrendered for repayable tax credits.

If, however, it had a loss of £150,000, only £112,500 would be attributable to enhanced R&D expenditure, which could be surrendered for repayable tax credits.

In the latter case, if the £112,500 loss were surrendered, tax credits of £12,375 (£112,500 x 11%) would be repaid, which is 24.75% of the actual £50,000 spent.

Deduction 73. Sub-contracted R&D expenditure

Sub-contracted R&D for both companies and unincorporated businesses will still qualify for relief under general principles, if it's treated as an expense in the accounts and is incurred wholly and exclusively for the purposes of the business.

For companies there are, however, restrictions on the amount that will qualify for enhancement and the amount that can be included in a surrendered loss to obtain tax credits.

For SMEs the maximum amount that can be enhanced and included in a loss surrendered for tax credits is 65% of the costs incurred if the company and the sub-contractor are unconnected, or the sub-contractor's costs if they are connected.

For large companies, expenditure on sub-contracted R&D will generally only qualifying for enhancement if it is sub-contracted to an individual, a partnership comprising only individuals, a charity or a higher education institution.

Where a large company (or an SME R&D sub-contractor) sub-contracts work to an SME, the sub-contractor SME's expenditure on the R&D effectively falls under the large company scheme (30% enhancement and no repayable tax credits available). R&D sub-contracted by a large company to another large company will be qualifying expenditure for the sub-contractor.

Deduction 74. R&D capital allowances

R&D capital allowances (RDAs) are available for expenditure on capital items used in R&D; the equipment used in the R&D work and even the buildings in which it's carried on.

An allowance of 100% of the qualifying expenditure can be claimed, but only in the period in which the expenditure is incurred. However, where expenditure is incurred before the relevant trade commences, it is treated as having been incurred in the first period of trading.

It isn't necessary to claim the whole 100% allowance if it isn't required (although the circumstances in which you wouldn't are limited), but there's a quirk in the legislation for RDAs. If the 100% allowance is fully claimed there won't be a balancing charge if the capital items concerned are subsequently disposed of, but if the allowance is only partially claimed, a balancing charge will arise on disposal.

Research and development

CHAPTER 7

Bad debts, losses and other accounting adjustments

For the purposes of tax, the profits should usually be calculated using normal accountancy practice. Things like depreciation and amortisation (except where the intangibles rules in Chapter 5 apply), can't be deducted for tax purposes though.

Deduction 75. Business tax deduction for bad debts

Where it becomes clear that a particular debtor isn't going to pay and either it isn't economically practicable to pursue the debt or the expectation of recovery is remote, the debt can be written off in the accounts of a business, and can be treated as a tax deductible expense in calculating its taxable profits.

If a debt that has been written off in this way is subsequently recovered, an adjustment will be needed, at that time, to reverse the tax relief effect that had been previously obtained.

EXAMPLE

Clipsie Ltd is owed £1,000 by a private individual who it has been unable to trace. Clipsie decides that it's no longer worthwhile and writes the amount off in its accounts for the year ended December 31 2011, thus obtaining tax relief for the bad debt. The profits that are taxed are £1,000 less than they would have been.

In mid-December 2012 the company's solicitors, who had originally been chasing a debt, receive a payment on the company's behalf from the individual of £800.

In its accounts to December 31 2012, Clipsie includes a negative bad debt of £800. Now £800 more profits are taxed than would have been the case, offsetting the tax relief obtained in the previous year on the £800 that has now been recovered.

Deduction 76. Business tax deduction for monetary losses

Similarly, where a business suffers a monetary loss, perhaps due to burglary or theft by an employee, the amount lost can be deducted from taxable business profits, to the extent that it isn't recoverable under an insurance policy.

However, it isn't permissible to deduct monetary losses arising from a misappropriation by a director or anyone in a proprietorial capacity (a business partner that absconds for example) in this way.

Deduction 77. Business tax deduction for stock losses

Likewise, any loss of stock through fraud or damage will give rise to a tax deduction. This will generally be automatic, as the lost stock will simply not be included in the closing stock valuation. An adjustment will, however, need to be made for any insurance proceeds.

Farsight Ltd has recently had to dispose of some stock that was damaged by a water leak in their warehouse. The damaged stock cost £10,000, but the company was only able to recover £5,000 under its insurance, so has lost £5,000 overall.

During the month to June 30 2012 when the damage happened, Farsight had purchased stock of £50,000 and sold stock with a cost of £80,000 for £120,000. Farsight had stock costing £150,000 at the beginning of June.

If the stock hadn't been lost, Farsight's closing stock figure would have been £120,000 (£150,000 + £50,000 - £80,000) and its gross profit would have been:

	£	£
Sales		120,000
Opening stock	150,000	
Purchases	50,000	
Closing stock	(120,000)	
Cost of sales		(80,000)
		40,000

As a result of the lost stock, the closing stock figure will be £10,000 lower at £110,000 and the gross profit will actually be:

	£	£
Sales		120,000
Opening stock	150,000	
Purchases	50,000	
Insurance receipt	(5,000)	
Closing stock	(110,000)	
Cost of sales		(85,000)
Gross profit		35,000

The reduced stock valuation and insurance adjustment mean that tax relief for the overall £5,000 loss relating to the damaged stock will be obtained automatically.

Deduction 78. VAT adjustments for bad debts and losses

Bad debt relief is available for VAT purposes as well.

For anyone that operates a cash basis of accounting for VAT, relief will be obtained automatically, because output VAT will not have to be paid over to the VATman until the debt has been paid.

For those not on a cash basis, who have to pay the VAT over to the VATman as they raise invoices, they need a means of recovering the VAT that they've charged on any VAT-inclusive invoices that they've raised and which haven't been paid.

For VAT purposes, it's possible to make a VAT adjustment for this VAT by making a corresponding increase in the input VAT due for a later period once:

- a period of six months has elapsed; and

- the debt has been written of in the accounts/books of the business.

Where a debt is partially paid, the payment is assumed to be applied on a VAT-inclusive basis.

EXAMPLE

Maugrim Ltd issued an invoice to a customer for £1,800 (£1,500, plus £300 VAT) on June 15 2012. The company is now preparing its accounts for the year ended December 31 2012 and only £600 of the debt has been paid by the customer.

The company believes that it's unlikely to recover the remaining £1,200 debt and is writing it off in its accounts. The £600 paid is assumed to contain an element of VAT (£600 x 1/6th = £100) and so the outstanding amount comprises a £1,000 sales value and £200 VAT.

Now that the debt is more than six months old and has been written off in the books, Maugrim can add £200 to the amount of input VAT that it claims on its next VAT return.

Again, if after making the adjustment any amount of the debt is recovered, a corresponding addition to the output VAT on the next VAT return should be made to reflect the VAT amount that has since been recovered.

In respect of losses, any input VAT will have been claimed on the purchase of stock at the time of purchase, and no adjustment will be necessary and monetary losses will generally have no effect. If takings are lost or stolen after a sale has been made, the output VAT included in the sale will still need to be paid to the VATman.

Deduction 79. Specific bad debt provisions

Just like actual bad debts it's often appropriate for accounting purposes to make prudent allowance for any amount of debtors that it's anticipated are unlikely to be paid. This allowance is often referred to as a bad debt provision.

To the extent that this bad debt provision is made up of an allowance for specific debts and there is reasonable evidence to support the view that recovery is doubtful, the Taxman accepts that the amount can also be deducted for the purposes of calculating taxable profits.

If the debt is subsequently recovered, there will then need to be an adjustment to reverse the effect of the tax relief obtained, but this should generally be an automatic accounting effect.

Deduction 80. General bad debt provisions

Historically, the Taxman has not accepted what is often termed a general bad debt provision; that doesn't identify with particular debts and is often calculated as percentages of the total debts of differing ages.

For companies, however, the legislation was changed a few years ago to refer to impairment losses, rather than bad debts and debts estimated to be bad. This change of language reflects the modern accounting terminology.

From a technical accounting point of view, the term provision is really a misnomer, since accounting standards define a provision as a liability of uncertain timing or amount, and impairment loss is actually the correct term.

In his internal manuals, the Taxman accepts that an impairment loss calculated in accordance with the Financial Reporting Standard (FRS) 26, will qualify for deduction. FRS 26 doesn't apply to many companies, but an impairment loss can still be calculated according to FRS 26, so that tax relief will be obtained.

Significantly, FRS 26 makes the point that, whilst any impairment loss that is calculated based on formulae might not relate to specific amounts, it nonetheless represents specific bad debts, which have simply not yet been individually identified.

In order to obtain full relief, the bad debt provision should be correctly renamed as an impairment loss and calculated in accordance with FRS 26.

The FRS 26 calculation is a three-stage process:

- material items should be identified and individually assessed for the prospects of their recovery
- the remaining debts should be separated into groups according to their risk characteristics
- the groups identified should be assessed collectively using estimates of recoverability based on empirical evidence, which should be constantly revised.

Typically, a company's individually immaterial debtors will have common risk characteristics, meaning that the process is not significantly different from the classic bad debt provision calculation.

Whilst the Taxman makes no acknowledgement, the inference is that an FRS 26 impairment loss should also be deductible from taxable business profits for an unincorporated business.

Deduction 81. Stock provisions

Accounting standards require that a business includes stock in its accounts at the lower of cost and net realisable value.

Where stock remains unsold or excess stock levels are held, it's appropriate to make an adjustment to reduce its value (at cost) to the amount expected to be realised after taking account of the costs of selling or disposing of the stock.

This has historically been called an obsolete or slow moving stock provision, which, in the past, has caused the Taxman to seek to prevent the adjustment from being deducted from taxable profits. Once again, these amounts are more correctly described in modern accounting parlance as impairment losses.

Whatever it's called, this reduction in value is correctly tax deductible and tax relief should be achieved by simply reducing the closing stock valuation by the amount of the adjustment. It will work in exactly the same way as the example in Deduction 75.

Deduction 82. Provisions for liabilities and accounting estimates

The Taxman's internal manuals confirm that a provision for a liability will be deductible provided it conforms to accounting standards.

The current relevant accounting standard is the FRS 12, which defines a provision as a liability of uncertain timing or amount, and permits the inclusion of a provision in the accounts if:

- there is a current obligation
- as a result of a past event
- to transfer future economic benefits (usually payment)
- which can be reliably estimated.

It says that the current obligation may be either a legal or a constructive obligation and that a constructive obligation will generally arise once the business has made some sort of public statement that it intends to act in a certain way.

Examples of provisions that are often made, and which are tax allowable are:

- for future repair work on leased premises where the tenant is bound under the lease to put right any dilapidations before the lease terminates

- for future repairs to products manufactured under product warranty obligations; and

- for redundancy and other costs on closure of sites/branches, once a public statement has been made that those sites/branches will be closed.

Download Zone

For an **Obligation of Past Event document**, visit **http://books.indicator.co.uk**. You'll find the access code on page 2 of this book.

CHAPTER 8

Travel, accommodation and subsistence

Expenditure on travel, accommodation and subsistence will generally be allowable, but it's an area in which there has been a fair amount of case law. This means that there are now some complex rules to navigate, which are examined in this chapter.

The input VAT incurred on any business travel, accommodation or subsistence expenses can also be recovered. Where such expenses are incurred by the employee and reimbursed by the employer, the employer will be permitted to recover the input VAT.

Deduction 83. Itinerant business travel for directors and employees

Employees (including directors) will usually have one or more normal places of work.

Where the duties of their employment involve them in travel that is itinerant (a travelling salesperson for example) or that otherwise takes them away from their normal place(s) of work, the cost of the travel will be an allowable expense to deduct from their earnings. Where the employer reimburses such expenses, they will be deductible in calculating the taxable business profits.

This will be the case even if the journey concerned commences from or ends at their home.

EXAMPLE

Ruth is a director of an incorporated firm of architects, which has an office. She regularly has to go out to visit clients and make site visits in the surrounding area. Ruth lives 30 miles away from her office.

When she makes a visit first thing in the morning, she travels directly from her home and when she makes a visit last thing in the afternoon she travels straight back home afterwards without first visiting the office.

All of Ruth's travel expenses in these circumstances are allowable expenses that can be deducted from her employment income.

Deduction 84. Itinerant business travel for the self-employed

Similarly, the self-employed will usually have one or more places where they normally carry on their self-employment.

In exactly the same way as employees, if their work is itinerant in nature or takes them away from their normal base(s), the cost of the travel will be deductible, even if the journey starts and ends at home.

The travel expenses in the above example of Ruth would have been deductible in calculating Ruth's self-employed profits if she had been self-employed.

Deduction 85. Travel between permanent workplaces for directors and employees

Where a director has more than one permanent workplace and they need to travel between the two, the travel expenses will be allowable and any reimbursement by the employer will be deductible in calculating their business profits liable to tax.

However, this won't apply if one of the permanent workplaces is their home. The cost of travel from home to a permanent workplace is always considered to be ordinary commuting and never allowable; neither will any journey that is substantially ordinary commuting. The cost also can't be made allowable by making a slight detour for some minor incidental purpose.

A permanent workplace may be a specific location or an area and a permanent workplace will be any place:

- where the employee spends more than 40% of their working time and where they have worked (or expect in total to work) for a continuous period of 24 months (or the duration of the employment if shorter)
- that represents the base from which the duties of the employment are performed, and which the employee attends regularly
- which the employee attends regularly and where the tasks of the employment are allocated
- that the employee regularly works at that isn't a temporary workplace.

Where the permanent workplace is an area, travel around the area is also an allowable expense. This doesn't mean that if the employee lives within the area there won't be any non-allowable ordinary commuting costs, if the day's work begins and ends in the area.

EXAMPLE

Fred is a travelling salesman of office supplies for Hogglestock Ltd, which has its head office in Northampton. Fred is based at the company's warehouse in Bicester and lives in Towcester.

Every Friday morning Fred travels to the head office for a sales meeting where targets for the following week are set. He then travels to the Bicester warehouse where he spends the afternoon doing paperwork.

On a Monday morning Fred first goes to the Bicester warehouse to complete any paperwork from the previous week and in order to collect samples. Monday afternoon through to Thursday is spent travelling.

The company's head office (where Fred's tasks are allocated and which he attends regularly) is a permanent workplace. So is the Bicester warehouse, which again Fred attends regularly and which is the base from which Fred performs his employment duties.

Fred's travel to Northampton on Friday mornings is ordinary commuting and the costs of it are not allowable, but the expenses of the journey from Northampton to Bicester after the meeting will be allowable.

Whilst the Northampton to Bicester journey takes him past his home along his Towcester to Northampton commute, it extends beyond Towcester to Bicester and so isn't substantially ordinary commuting, hence the allowable expenses.

Similarly, the costs of Fred's Monday morning journey from home to the Bicester warehouse (as well as the reverse journey on Friday evenings) are non-allowable ordinary commuting.

The expenses of Fred's remaining itinerant travelling will be allowable.

Deduction 86. Travel to temporary workplaces for directors and employees

Additionally, the costs of travelling to a temporary workplace can also be deducted from the employee's or director's employment income and for which employer reimbursements will be tax deductible.

A temporary workplace is a place where the employee attends for the purpose of performing a task of limited duration or for some other temporary purpose, and which isn't otherwise a permanent workplace.

In the example in Deduction 83 Ruth's visits might arguably be those to temporary workplaces, rather than itinerant travel.

Deduction 87. Travel between bases of operation for the self-employed

Apart from the fact that there's not a set of statutory rules, the rules for the deductibility of travel expenses from taxable business profits for the self-employed are not dissimilar to those set out in Deductions 85 and 86 for directors and employees.

The concept of a permanent workplace is replaced with the concept of a base of operations, but it's again possible to have more than one base of operations, and a base of operations can also be an area, rather than a specific place.

A base of operations is a place at which the person actually carries on their self-employment. It has, however, been held in case law that simply doing tasks at home that could be performed anywhere, paperwork in particular, isn't sufficient to make it a base of operations, unless there is no other place that is the base of operations.

Travel from home to a base of operations is not a deductible business expense though, even if sufficient self-employed activity is carried on there to make it a base of operations. Again, stopping or diverting en route for a minor incidental purpose won't change the nature of the journey from being considered commuting.

Examples of bases of operations from case law are:

- the chambers of a barrister, who also worked on cases at home
- the delivery round of a milkman; and
- the market in question in the case of a market trader.

George is a self-employed proprietor of two hardware shops in Scunthorpe and Grimsby. George has employees who run the shops and he spends half of his time at each shop. He writes his books up at his home in Grimsby. The journey from Grimsby to Scunthorpe is around 40 miles.

The two shops are George's bases of operations. His home isn't even though he writes the books up there.

When he travels to either shop from home that is a non-allowable commuting journey, but the cost of the journeys between the two shops are allowable. Clearly George will be better off starting and ending his day at the Grimsby shop.

If he only pops into the Grimsby shop for some fleeting purpose when travelling between home and the Scunthorpe shop, the cost of his journey to or from Scunthorpe will remain non-allowable as commuting.

Deduction 88. Travel to temporary sites for the self-employed

In exactly the same way as for employees and directors, someone who is self-employed may travel to places at which they only work temporarily. The cost of such travel will be allowable in calculating their taxable business profits.

EXAMPLE

John is a bricklayer who works at various building sites as demand for his services is required. He typically works at any one site for a period of between a few days and a few months and may carry out work at several different sites at different times.

John writes up his books at home, where he also keeps his tools and where contractors contact him to engage his services.

John has no other base of operations, and so his home will be regarded as his base of operations and the costs of travel to the various different sites can be deducted when he calculates his taxable business profits.

For the self-employed there are no set rules as to what period of time and amount of time spent working at a place will render it a permanent base of operations, rather than merely a temporary site. Case law is still developing in this area, but in cases of doubt it's advisable to apply the 24-month rule for employees.

This broadly means that if a person is spending (or expects in total to spend) more than 40% of their time over a continuous period of 24 months (or the duration of the wider self-employment if shorter) at one site, then that site should probably be regarded as a permanent base of operations.

Deduction 89. Overnight accommodation for directors and employees

Where business travel takes a director or employee away from home and it's then necessary that they stay overnight, the cost of overnight accommodation will be an allowable expense that the director or employee can deduct from their earnings, if they bear the expense. Reimbursements by the employer will also be tax deductible for them.

If the employer bears the cost of overnight accommodation, there will be no benefit in kind on the employee.

Deduction 90. Overnight incidental expenses for directors and employees

Where a director or employee does need to stay away overnight an employer can (in addition to their accommodation and subsistence costs) pay them a flat allowance for each night of their stay away that will be tax deductible for the employer, but non-taxable for the employee.

The amount is £5 per night for UK overnight stays and £10 per night for overnight stays outside the UK.

No input VAT can be claimed by the employer in respect of these amounts, however.

Download Zone

For an **Incidental Overnight Expenses Policy**, visit **http://books.indicator. co.uk**. You'll find the access code on page 2 of this book.

Deduction 91. Living accommodation for directors and employees

Where an employer provides an employee (including a director) with living accommodation the cost will be tax deductible for the employer, but there may be a benefit in kind for the employee.

The amount of the benefit will usually be the rental cost of making the accommodation available to the employee if the employer rents it or the property's rateable value plus an amount of notional interest computed at the Taxman's official rate on the amount by which the cost of the property exceeds £75,000.

There will be no benefit on the employee, where the accommodation is provided:

- for the proper performance of their employment duties
- for the better performance of their employment duties and it's customary for accommodation to be provided to employees in employment of that kind

8

- as part of special security arrangements due to a special security threat to the employee; or
- in the circumstances described in Deduction 92.

The first two bulleted items do not, however, apply to directors who have a material interest (greater than 5%) in their employer companies and will not apply if the director does not work full time.

Deduction 92. Non-taxable living accommodation for directors and employees

Where an employee incurs an expense on living accommodation in circumstances where it's a substitute for allowable overnight accommodation, and the cost doesn't exceed the cost that would have been spent on such accommodation, it will be allowable from the employee's taxable earnings.

Similarly, where the employer bears the expense of providing such accommodation the employee will be entitled to deduct a notional expense that is equal and opposite to the benefit that would otherwise arise as described in Deduction 91.

EXAMPLE

David lives in Brighton and his employer, Coriakin Ltd, is sending him on a six-month secondment to their Manchester office.

Since it's too long a distance for David to commute daily, Coriakin is renting a flat for him in Manchester at a cost of £750 per month for him to stay in overnight during the week. This is less than the £50 per night hotel cost that they would otherwise incur.

On three occasions David and his wife stayed in the flat at weekends while they were visiting friends in the area. These stays did not result in any additional cost for Coriakin.

The total accommodation cost for the six-month secondment is £4,500, which is taxable as a benefit in kind on David, but he has a corresponding notional expense deduction to set against this, meaning that overall there is no taxable benefit.

The personal use of the flat does not give rise to a benefit or a restriction in the notional expense deduction as there was no additional expense attributable to this personal use.

Deduction 93. Overnight accommodation for the self-employed

Similarly, for the self-employed, where the business travel requires that they stay away from home overnight, the cost of overnight accommodation will be deductible from their taxable business profits.

In circumstances where there is an extended stay away, the cost of living accommodation would be a tax deductible expense in the same way as applied to employees in Deduction 92.

Deduction 94. Subsistence expenses for directors and employees

Where an employee is travelling away from their normal workplace or where the duties of their employment mean that they are itinerant, the cost of any subsistence expenses incurred will be deductible from their employment income. The same applies to subsistence costs incurred while staying away overnight on business.

Subsistence expenses will not be deductible from the employment income where the employee is staying in living accommodation, such that they are in a home-from-home position.

Where actual subsistence costs are reimbursed by the employer, the employer is able to recover any input VAT and the amount reimbursed will be deductible.

Deduction 95. Flat rate subsistence allowances for directors and employees

As an alternative to Deduction 94, an employer can agree with the Taxman to pay flat rate subsistence allowances to employees where they have evidence of having incurred costs for subsistence. In this respect, the Taxman has published what he calls benchmark rates that can be adopted by employers by simply notifying him.

The rates are £5 where the absence from the normal place of work (or the itinerant day) is at least five hours and £10 where it is at least ten hours.

Additionally, if exceptionally the employee has to be away earlier than 6am, a £5 amount for breakfast is allowed and if they are exceptionally away later than 8pm, a £15 late evening meal allowance can be paid.

Alternatively, the employer can reimburse actual amounts, which may be preferable when the actual amounts are higher.

Where flat rate amounts are paid they will be tax deductible for the employer, but no input VAT can be recovered.

Download Zone

For a **Scale Rate Clearance Letter**, visit **http://books.indicator.co.uk**. You'll find the access code on page 2 of this book.

Deduction 96. Subsistence for the self-employed

The cost of a self-employed individual's sustenance is not generally deductible from their taxable business profits.

However, where a self-employed person is itinerant or is travelling outside their normal pattern, they are permitted to deduct costs incurred on subsistence in calculating the taxable profits. Costs of subsistence where an overnight stay is required are also deductible.

However, if the individual is staying in living accommodation, so that they are in a home-from-home position, the subsistence costs are not then a permitted deduction.

Deduction 97. Overseas travel for spouses, partners and children

Where an employee is performing the duties of their employment outside the UK for a period of at least 60 days, then the employer can pay for or reimburse the costs of a journey for their spouse, civil partner or child to go with, visit or come back with the employee.

The amount paid or reimbursed in this way will be a taxable benefit or expense for the employee, but they will have a corresponding expense deduction of the same amount, so that, overall, none of the amount is chargeable to tax.

Deduction 98. Holidays for directors and employees

Where a business trip for a director or employee is combined with a holiday, the cost will be tax deductible for the employer, but the employee or director will have a benefit in kind (which will be the cost to the employer of providing the trip (inclusive of VAT).

If the business trip was an essential, rather than incidental, part of the journey, it should be possible to reduce the amount of the benefit by the proportion of the costs properly attributable to that purpose.

Deduction 99. Holidays for the self-employed

Similarly for the self-employed, where, as an incidence of an essential business trip overseas, there is a private excursion, the cost of the business trip, excluding any additional amount for the private excursion, can be deducted in calculating the taxable profits of the business.

Where, however, the business trip is in reality incidental to some private purpose, none of the costs of the trip will be tax deductible.

CHAPTER 9

Training, conferences and seminars

The cost of training, conferences and seminars for proprietors and employees will be deductible from taxable business profits and any input VAT will usually be recoverable. However, there are some specific points to be aware of which are covered in this chapter.

Deduction 100. Training provided to directors and employees

Where a company provides training or reimburses employees for the cost of training, any VAT incurred will be recoverable and the costs will be a tax deductible business expense.

No benefit in kind will arise on the employee though, provided the training concerned is a course or other activity designed to impart, instil, improve or reinforce any knowledge, skills or personal qualities which:

- are likely to prove useful to the employee when performing the duties of the employment; or
- will better qualify the employee to perform those duties.

> EXAMPLE
>
> Richard employs his son Michael in his small car hire business. Michael can't currently drive and it would be useful both to the business and to Michael in doing his job if he could.
>
> Accordingly, the company pays for Michael to learn to drive. The costs are tax deductible for the company and any input VAT incurred is recoverable, but there's no benefit in kind for either Michael or Richard.
>
> Because Michael is Richard's son, the costs might not have been tax deductible if Richard's business were not incorporated, because the Taxman would have argued that they weren't wholly and exclusively for the purposes of the business.

Where, however, the employee incurs training costs that aren't reimbursed by the employer, they will not normally be deductible from their employment income.

Deduction 101. Training costs for the self-employed

The cost of training for a self-employed proprietor of a business (or any family member who works in the business) will be deductible if it's incurred wholly and exclusively for the purposes of the business (so that there's no personal purpose of the expenditure, as might be the case in the Richard and Michael example in Deduction 100).

Where, however, any training for a self-employed proprietor brings about new expertise or knowledge, or leads to a recognised qualification, the Taxman considers that it isn't a tax deductible business expense.

9

Deduction 102. Travel for training for directors and employees

Where an employer pays for or reimburses travel costs in relation to training, the treatment follows that set out for the training itself in Deduction 100.

Where an employee incurs travelling expenses that the employer doesn't reimburse, the costs are not deductible from their employment earnings.

Deduction 103. Travel for training for the self-employed

Similarly, any travel costs that would be tax deductible under Chapter 8 for a self-employed proprietor if the training were an activity of the self-employment, will be tax deductible if the costs of the training would also be deductible as set out in Deduction 101.

Deduction 104. Overseas conferences and seminars for directors and employees

If it's necessary within the confines of the employment for a director or employee to attend an overseas conference or seminar, the cost will be tax deductible for the employer, any input VAT can be recovered and there will not be a benefit in kind for the employee. However, where an employee bears the expense, it will only be allowable if attendance at the seminar or conference is necessary in order to carry out the duties of the employment.

Deduction 105. Accompanying partners on overseas events for directors and employees

Sometimes it may be beneficial for a director or employee's spouse or partner to accompany them on an overseas business event. If the employer pays for or reimburses the cost, it will be a tax deductible business expense, but the employee or director will have a benefit in kind.

They will then be entitled to a corresponding expense deduction in the following circumstances:

- the spouse or partner has some special skill or qualification (such as an interpreter) associated with the duties that the director or employee will be performing that will be needed on the trip (although not necessarily full-time)
- the presence of the spouse or partner is essential to host a series of business entertaining occasions that the director or employee will be required to organise as part of their duties
- the employee's health is poor, so that it would be unreasonable for them to travel alone.

Deduction 106. Overseas conferences and seminars for the self-employed

Where the cost of attendance at an overseas conference or seminar are incurred wholly and exclusively for the purposes of a self-employed business, they will be a tax deductible business expense. Similar considerations need to be given to those referred to in the context of holidays under Deduction 99 in Chapter 8.

Deduction 107. Accompanying partners on overseas events for the self-employed

Where attendance at an overseas seminar or conference is necessary for a self-employment, the cost of a spouse or partner accompanying the self-employed proprietor will be a tax deductible business expense, if they too are incurred wholly and exclusively for the purposes of the business.

Similar considerations to those in Deduction 105 will apply in this respect.

CHAPTER 10

Entertaining

The provision of business entertainment, including hospitality of any kind, is not generally an allowable business or employment expense and the associated input VAT is also blocked from recovery. The following deductions highlight the exceptions to this general rule.

There are similar restrictions for gifts, the exceptions to which are looked at in Chapter 11.

Deduction 108. Entertaining for promotional purposes

Where hospitality or entertainment is provided in order to advertise to the public generally, and they are things that the business (usually in the hospitality industry) normally supplies, then the cost of providing that hospitality or entertainment is an allowable business expense. However, input VAT can't be recovered in these circumstances.

EXAMPLE

Ilgamuth Ltd has recently acquired a new public house for its portfolio of branded pubs that provide a standard range of bar meals. The pub had been in disuse when purchased and the first month's trading following refurbishment is still disappointing.

In order to raise public awareness that the pub has been refurbished and reopened, Ilgamuth stages an open afternoon to which the local press, immediate local community and a number of local dignitaries (in order to increase press interest) are invited. Food and drinks (alcoholic and non-alcoholic) are provided on the open afternoon.

Since the food and drink are part of their normal business to supply, and because they have been provided at the open afternoon for the purposes of advertising to the public generally, the costs of providing these are an allowable business expense, but the input VAT on the costs is blocked from recovery.

Deduction 109. Entertaining staff

The provision of hospitality and entertainment to the staff of a business (and others for whom the provision is incidental to the staff provision) is an allowable business expense, but is likely to give rise to a benefit in kind for the staff concerned.

There's no benefit in kind for staff if the entertainment is provided at an annual party or similar function and the cost per head (or the function together with other similar ones to which this exemption is to be applied) does not exceed £150 (including VAT). The whole amount will be taxable on the employees if the (VAT inclusive) £150 per head limit is exceeded.

Input VAT will be recoverable on the costs of providing staff, including directors and managers with hospitality or entertainment, but not for any guests. If the only attendees are people who stand in a proprietorial capacity (such as owner-managers) and their guests, however, the input VAT can't be recovered.

Pittencream Ltd has 14 members who each take a guest to the Christmas dinner and party. The shareholder-director Eustace Scrubb and his wife also attend. The total cost of the Christmas dinner and party is £3,000, plus £600 VAT.

30 people attended in total and the VAT-inclusive cost is £3,600, which is £120 per head. Since this is less than the £150 threshold, neither Eustace nor any of the employees will have a benefit in kind.

Input VAT can't be recovered in respect of Eustace's wife or the other 14 guests. The only input VAT that can be recovered is in respect of Eustace and the 14 employees, i.e. £300 (£600 x 15/30). The remaining £300 is blocked from recovery.

The cost to the company, after the irrecoverable VAT, of £3,300 is an allowable business expense.

If Pittencream had no employees other than Eustace, the company could still have paid for an event for Eustace and his wife of up to £300 (VAT inclusive). There still wouldn't be a benefit in kind for Eustace, but the input VAT attributable to his share of the event would not then be recoverable.

Where hospitality or entertainment is provided to staff in such a way that it's incidental to the provision of hospitality or entertainment to non-staff, its cost will not, however, be an allowable business expense and input VAT recovery will be blocked.

The provision or reimbursement of accommodation and subsistence to employees and independent contractors who are akin to employees will also not be considered business entertainment and input VAT can be recovered. For employees though, the provision or reimbursement may strictly be a taxable expense or benefit, but an expense deduction may be possible.

Deduction 110. Entertaining under a contractual obligation

If a business is in some way contractually bound to provide hospitality or entertainment, it will not constitute business entertainment and so will be an allowable business expense. Input VAT can be recovered if the nature of the contractual obligation is such that the hospitality or entertainment forms part of a business supply for which consideration is being received.

Wimbleweather Ltd provides various training courses to businesses. Tea and coffee is provided on arrival, plus mid-morning and mid-afternoon. Lunch is also laid on. The prices of the courses are set to take account of these costs, and would-be delegates are advised, in the company's promotional material, that lunch and refreshments during the day are included.

The company is under a contractual obligation to provide the lunch and refreshments and these are incorporated into its VAT supply of a training course. Accordingly, the provision doesn't represent business entertainment; the costs of providing the lunch and refreshments are an allowable business expense and input VAT can be recovered on them.

Deduction 111. Entertaining under a reciprocal obligation

Similarly, where a business has an obligation to provide hospitality that is reciprocal in nature it will not constitute business entertainment, and will be an allowable business expense. Input VAT will be recoverable if the expenditure has been incurred on hospitality and entertainment under the obligation for the purposes of making business supplies.

EXAMPLE

Go Surround Limited is a member of a local trade association established for the purpose of promoting business in the local area and political lobbying. Under the rules of the trade association, members are required to take their turn at hosting monthly meetings and providing light refreshments to the attendees. Go Surround is hosting the next meeting of the trade association.

Since, under the rules of the trade association, Go Surround is required to take its turn at hosting, and since this will be reciprocated by other members of the trade association, the provision of light refreshments by Go Surround at the next meeting will not be considered business entertainment and will be allowable.

Since Go Surround will be incurring the costs of the provision under a reciprocal obligation for the purposes of its business, and, therefore, for making business supplies, it will be able to recover the VAT on those costs.

Deduction 112. Entertaining where there is quid pro quo

The Taxman also accepts that expenditure on providing hospitality isn't business entertainment where there is, what he calls, "quid pro quo" (where the recipient provides services of value in exchange).

EXAMPLE

Lucy is a freelance journalist researching a series of articles on the widget manufacturing industry. Andrew has a wealth of experience in widget manufacturing and is considered to be something of an industry expert. Lucy offers to take Andrew for a light lunch if he will provide some detailed insight into the industry to help her with her series of articles.

The cost of taking Andrew to lunch will not be business entertainment, because he is providing Lucy with quid pro quo, and so the expense is allowable and Lucy can recover the input VAT.

Deduction 113. Input VAT on entertaining overseas customers

Input VAT is recoverable in respect of expenditure incurred on entertaining overseas customers if it's of a reasonable scale and not unnecessarily lavish.

However, the VATman expects output VAT to be accounted for on the cost of the private benefit received by the customer, unless there's a strict business purpose for the expenditure (such as sandwiches for a lunchtime meeting).

Hospitality for overseas customers outside of the workplace (but not in restaurants) will also not necessitate output VAT being accounted for on a private benefit if it's of a similar nature and scale to that which might be provided at the workplace and doesn't involve alcohol.

There's no need to account for output VAT on a private benefit if the input VAT hasn't been recovered.

Deduction 114. Entertaining as an employment expense for directors and employees

Entertaining expenditure incurred by an employee or director is subject to the same limitations - an expense deduction won't generally be available unless it falls within one of the above exceptions.

However, if the expenditure is reimbursed by the employer or funded by way of an expense advance that would otherwise be taxable as earnings, the deduction is permitted if the employer doesn't seek relief for the expenditure when computing their business profits.

CHAPTER 11

Advertising, promotion, gifts, samples and sponsorship

Expenditure for promoting the business (including expenditure on gifts and samples) can normally be deducted, and input VAT will normally be recoverable.

Where expenditure relating to the promotion of the employer's business is incurred by an employee, the expense will be deductible from their employment income.

There are some restrictions and the major types of item that will qualify and the restrictions, where they apply, are set out in the following deductions.

Deduction 115. Advertising

Most expenditure of an advertising nature incurred for the purposes of the business will be deductible. This will include things such as:

- placing an ad in the Yellow Pages or similar

- advertising goods or services in a trade or speciality magazine

- advertising for staff

- radio, television and Internet advertising.

There are, however, some special rules covering sponsorship, promotional events and gifts and samples that are considered below.

Deduction 116. Promotional events

Expenditure on events held for the purposes of promoting or developing a business is allowable deduction to the extent that it does not represent business entertainment.

EXAMPLE

Moonwood Ltd is holding an event to mark the company's birthday, at which it will launch a number of new products. It's hiring a venue to make its intended presentation of the new products and provide catering for the 100 attendees. This will cost £1,200 (VAT inclusive) for the venue and facilities and £240 (VAT inclusive) for the catering.

It's also hiring the services of a string quartet at a cost of £480 (VAT inclusive).

Overall, the event is for the purposes of promoting the business, but the expenditure on catering and the string quartet is for the purposes of business entertainment and is not deductible expenditure. Neither is the input VAT on these items recoverable.

Input VAT of £200 can be recovered on the hire of the venue and facilities and the net £1,000 cost is an expense that is deductible in the company's taxable business profits.

The Taxman's internal manuals also say that, for the purposes of calculating taxable business profits, expenditure on such an event can be deducted in full where the entertainment element is minimal. They give the example of an author's book launch where there is moderate provision of food and wine.

Deduction 117. Travel to promotional events

The provision of travel for an attendee of a promotional event is considered to be hospitality and so is non-allowable business entertainment.

Where employees or directors are paid expenses for travelling to such an event though, these costs are deductible business expenses and shouldn't give rise to any tax liability for the employee or director under general travel principles.

EXAMPLE

Peter is employed by Tumnus Ltd as a business development manager. The company has arranged a golf day for a number of its key customers, the expenditure on which will be non-allowable business entertaining. Peter claims for his mileage to and from the event, which Tumnus pays at the Taxman's approved rates.

Tumnus is allowed to deduct the expense in calculating its taxable business profits and the reimbursement will not be taxable employment income in Peter's hands.

Proprietors of an unincorporated business incurring expenditure on travelling to and from such an event that they are hosting will also be able to claim the costs.

Deduction 118. Networking events

A business may bear the cost of staff or proprietors attending networking events or employees may incur such expenses. These (together with any connected travel costs) will be allowable deductions, notwithstanding that the costs may contain an element of subsistence.

EXAMPLE

Peter, from the previous example, attends a monthly breakfast networking meeting which costs £15. Tumnus reimburses Peter the cost of the meeting and his mileage at the Taxman's approved rates.

The costs reimbursed by Tumnus are deductible from the company's taxable business profits and the mileage payment will not be taxable on Peter. The reimbursed networking expense is strictly a benefit for Peter, but he will have a corresponding expense deduction, so that there is no final amount taxable.

Even though there is a subsistence element that might not normally qualify as an employment expense, this is incidental to the main purpose of the expenditure, which is to attend the networking event in the performance of his employment duties.

Again, similar expenditure incurred by a proprietor of an unincorporated business would also be deductible.

Deduction 119. Promotional gifts

Expenditure on goods gifted by a business is generally precluded from qualifying as a deduction.

A deduction is allowed where the cost of the goods (together with any other qualifying gifts made to the same person in the same year) does not exceed £50, provided that the goods are not food, drink, tobacco or a token or voucher exchangeable for goods, and that they bear a conspicuous advertisement for the business.

EXAMPLE

Bricklethumb Ltd purchases a number of digital calendars, which include a panel bearing a small ad for the company. The calendars cost £35 (plus VAT) each and one is given to all their customers for Christmas. There have been no other gifts to the customers in the year.

The £7 VAT paid on each calendar is recoverable input VAT and the £35 net cost of each calendar is deductible.

Deduction 120. Samples

Where a business gives trade samples for the purposes of advertising or promotion, their cost is deductible.

EXAMPLE

Girbius Ltd is a widget manufacturer and is introducing a new speciality precision widget. It manufactures a number of prototypes at a cost of £80 per widget, which it gives to several of its key customers in the hope of generating sales.

The costs of manufacturing the prototype widgets (even though it exceeds £50 per recipient and doesn't bear a conspicuous ad) is a tax allowable business expense because the widgets are goods that it is the company's business to provide.

Deduction 121. Gifts to employees

The cost of goods given to employees can generally be deducted.

The gifts will normally be considered to be a benefit taxable on the employees (at their VAT-inclusive cost), unless the Taxman is prepared to accept that they are trivial (if what's received by each employee has a low cost).

Lilygloves Ltd provides each of its 50 employees and a handful of key customers a bottle of champagne each for Christmas. The cost for the employee is deductible, as the provision to customers is incidental to the provision for employees.

The Taxman will regard the provision of one bottle of champagne to each employee as a trivial benefit, so no tax liability will arise for them.

If the company had instead provided the champagne to 50 customers and just a handful of employees, none of the cost of the champagne would have been deductible for the company, since the provision to the employees is incidental to the provision to customers and there is no benefit in kind for the employees.

In practice, the Taxman will normally permit deduction of the expense where there is a benefit in kind taxable on the employees.

Deduction 122. Charitable gifts

The cost of goods gifted to charity will be eligible to be deducted from the taxable profits of the business if the goods were business trading stock. Gifts of plant or machinery of the business will also be treated as disposals at nil value and so will not give rise to a capital allowances balancing charge.

Deduction 123. Input VAT on gifts of goods and samples

Input VAT will generally be recoverable on goods that are to be gifted. However, the VAT-registered business will need to account for an equivalent amount of VAT at the time the goods are gifted, unless the gift is a qualifying business gift or a sample.

It's a qualifying business gift if the cost (taken together with other gifts to the same person in the preceding twelve months) doesn't exceed £50, and it's made for business purposes - including rewarding employees and promoting the business.

Note. For VAT purposes, there's no restriction for gifts of food, drink or tobacco and no requirement that the gift bears a conspicuous advertisement for the business.

Deduction 124. Input VAT on gifts of goods to charities

The treatment outlined in Deduction 123 above will also apply to any gifts of goods to charities. However, where the goods are being given to the charity for sale, export or letting, the supply will be zero-rated, meaning that no output VAT will be due but any input VAT can be recovered.

Deduction 125. Sponsorship

Expenditure on sponsorship for the purposes of promoting or advertising the business will generally be allowable, but it's an area that the Taxman is likely to examine closely.

The Taxman will look carefully at whether the expenditure has been incurred wholly and exclusively for the purposes of bringing promotional benefits to the business.

Where there is some personal benefit to the business proprietor, this is likely to give rise to a benefit in kind for a proprietor of an incorporated business. In the case of an unincorporated business the costs are unlikely to be allowable in these circumstances, particularly if the expenditure is determined by the needs of the promotional activity, rather than the needs of the business.

EXAMPLE

Susan runs a small equestrian business and participates in a number of show jumping events. Her husband runs a PR business which provides sponsorship of Susan's equestrian business in return for advertising and promotion at the show jumping events. The amount of sponsorship expenditure varies according to the needs of the equestrian business.

This is based on a real case in which it was held that the expenditure wasn't incurred wholly and exclusively for the purposes of the business, due to the combination of there being a personal relationship and the fact that the amount of sponsorship expenditure was determined according to the needs of the equestrian business rather than the promotional needs of the PR business.

There is, however, case law where the costs of a promotional activity were allowed where the activity was integral to and supportive of the business purposes.

EXAMPLE

Edmund is a self-employed mechanic and also participates in motor rallies. The expenses of his motor rallying are funded from his business.

The car he uses for rallying bears a number of advertisements for the business and is painted in the same livery as the van he uses for the business. His rallying success has also contributed positively to his business.

Again, this example is based on a real case where the expenditure of sponsoring the rallying activities was held to be an allowable deduction.

If Edmund operated through a limited company, there is likely to be a benefit in kind and the taxable proportion would probably need to be negotiated with the Taxman.

If the sponsorship activity brings about benefits that can be (and is) used to provide hospitality, there will usually be an apportionment of the expenditure to this hospitality element which may then be disallowed under the business entertainment rules.

EXAMPLE

Glimfeather Ltd has entered into a sponsorship arrangement with Narnia Rovers FC, under which Glimfeather will have an advertising board at the club's football ground and will be provided with the services of two of the club's players for half-day promotional events twice a year.

Glimfeather will also have the use of a box at five home matches each year. The sponsorship package costs £10,000 (plus VAT). A similar package without the box use option would have cost £8,000 (plus VAT).

During its year ended May 31 2013 (including the 2012/13 football season), Glimfeather uses it boxes for entertaining clients on three occasions and selected staff are allowed to use the box on the other two occasions.

The first £8,000 (net) is wholly attributable to genuine sponsorship and is a deductible expense in calculating the taxable profits of the business. The input VAT on this amount can also be recovered in full.

The remaining £2,000 (net) needs to be apportioned between the five occasions of use of the box. Twice it was used as a staff benefit, so £800 (£400 for each occasion) is attributable to that use. The £800 is again a deductible expense and the input VAT can be recovered on that amount.

The £400 amount will be apportioned between the staff who used the box on each occasion and taxed on them as a benefit in kind.

The remaining £1,200 of the £2,000 is attributable to entertaining. It's not a deductible expense in calculating the profits of the business and the input VAT on that amount can t be recovered.

Deduction 126. Input VAT on sponsorship

Input VAT will be recoverable on sponsorship where it's incurred for the purposes of the business, and so will generally follow the treatment for direct tax purposes.

Where there is a personal relationship between the business proprietor and the activity being sponsored, VAT case law has looked to see if there is some meaningful connection between the business activity and the activity being sponsored, either in terms of geography or the nature of the two activities.

CHAPTER 12

Fines, penalties, damages and compensation payments

The area of fines, penalties, damages and compensation payments presents a number of difficulties looked at in this chapter. As a general premise, the courts have been loath to allow a taxpayer to share the cost of any wrongdoing with the rest of taxpaying society, but the line where commercial success ends and wrongdoing begins is often blurred.

Deduction 127. Fines and penalties

Where a fine or penalty is imposed by the law (including local bylaws) it will not generally be a deductible expense. Where an employer pays such a fine or penalty for an employee it will be a deductible expense for the business, but will be a benefit in kind for the employee.

Penalties and fines imposed by government departments like HMRC, Companies House, the Information Commissioner and the Health and Safety Executive will not be tax deductible.

On the other hand, fines and penalties that arise under commercial arrangements (for late delivery/completion etc.), particularly where they are imposed contractually, are a normal incidence of business operation and will be a tax deductible expense.

Deduction 128. Parking and speeding fines, etc.

The area of fines relating to motoring offences is straightforward for the proprietor of an unincorporated business; they're simply not tax deductible. For an employer, however, a slightly more complex analysis is needed.

For example, parking fines are charged on the owner of the vehicle and won't, therefore, be allowable if the employer owns the vehicle.

However, speeding fines are charged on the driver. If an employer pays these or pays for parking fines for an employee's own vehicle, the employer will be entitled to a tax deduction, but the employee will have a benefit in kind.

Where parking fines don't relate to a breach of local bylaws - overstay charges in a privately run car park, for example - they may well arise under a contractual arrangement, meaning that they will be an allowable business expense.

Deduction 129. Damages and compensation

Payments of damages for loss, injury or damage arising as a consequence of the trade will usually be a tax deductible expense, provided they have not arisen out of any illegal activity.

There has been a recent case where damages for injury to a worker - where a fine was imposed by the Health and Safety Executive for a failure - was considered deductible despite the health and safety breach.

Another time that damages and compensation will not be deductible is if it's regarded as being capital in nature, because some asset of enduring benefit to the business arises. Damages and compensation are usually paid where a business seeks to free itself from obligations, so this generally won't be the case.

There is case law where payments to rid the business of a disadvantageous asset have been held to be non-allowable capital expenditure.

Deduction 130. Staff redundancy and termination payments

Any payment that arises out of termination of employment whether it be by redundancy or dismissal will be an allowable cost deductible from taxable business profits.

This will be the case even if unfair or wrongful dismissal is alleged. Compensation payments in these situations are ultimately of the nature of damages for breach of contract, as opposed to any wrongdoing on the part of the employer.

CHAPTER 13

Clothing, medical expenses and professional fees

This chapter focuses on a number of expenses that often have an intrinsic personal element. For proprietors of unincorporated businesses where any expense has such an element, it will not have been incurred wholly and exclusively for the purposes of the business and will not be tax deductible.

In a company or for employees of unincorporated businesses these sorts of costs will often give rise to a benefit in kind for the directors or employees affected.

Deduction 131. Protective clothing

Whilst clothing may often have some business need, it has been held by the courts that it will also serve the needs of the individual, which would prevent deduction (or give rise to a benefit in kind).

It's only when the needs of the business (or the employment duties for an employee) are the predominant purpose of an expense that it will be tax deductible.

Protective clothing, e.g. overalls and protective boots, is the most notable example of where this will be the case, and the proprietor of an unincorporated business will be able to obtain a full tax deduction for any protective clothing that they purchase for the purposes of their business.

Where directors of a company or employees are being provided with protective clothing, the cost will be fully deductible. Strictly, the employee or director will then have a benefit, but will be entitled to a corresponding expense deduction, so there's no overall benefit.

Deduction 132. Uniforms and specialist clothing

Likewise, where a trade or employment requires a uniform (or something amounting to a costume) to be worn, the cost will be fully deductible for the business.

EXAMPLE

Jason is a waiter in a stylish restaurant and he is provided with evening dress to wear whilst working in the restaurant. The provision of the evening dress to Jason by his employer is a benefit in kind, but he will be entitled to a corresponding expense deduction because it's his costume for his employment.

It is becoming increasingly common for businesses to adopt a corporate brand, which may involve staff dressing in a common style; unless the clothing is considered to be a uniform, the cost of the business providing it will not be allowable for the proprietor of an unincorporated business. It will be allowable for an employer, but will give rise to a benefit in kind.

To be considered a uniform each item of clothing will need to bear a conspicuous, non-removable badge or logo associated with the business. This will then mean that the cost or benefit of the uniform will be deductible as a business or employment expense.

Deduction 133. Laundry costs

Where the costs or benefits of any clothing are allowable as uniform or costume, then the reasonable costs of maintaining it, including laundry costs, will also be allowable.

Deduction 134. Flat rate laundry allowances for employees and directors

For employees and directors, the Taxman publishes scale rates for maintaining uniform/protective work clothing, which range from £60 to £140 per year, dependent on the type of industry that the employment is in.

For proprietors of unincorporated businesses it may be possible to agree with the Taxman to claim an annual deduction based on these scale rates.

Deduction 135. Medical bills and insurance

Generally speaking, any medical costs for the proprietor of an unincorporated business will not be tax deductible. For employees and directors, such costs will be taxable for the employer but will give rise to a benefit in kind for the employee or director.

There are situations where this won't apply. For example, there is a specific exemption for employed sportspeople who are injured playing sport and who need remedial treatment so that they can continue playing.

Likewise, for proprietors of unincorporated businesses there is case law where medical costs have been allowed (or would have been but for other factors). The most notable examples are:

- a television stuntman who was allowed the costs of remedial massage and physiotherapy as well as a private operation for an injury (that he could have had carried out on the NHS, but would have needed to wait while not being able to work in the intervening period)
- a guitar player who injured a finger and paid for surgery that he wouldn't have needed but for his guitar playing.

Deduction 136. Overseas medical treatment and insurance

Where directors and employees need to travel overseas for their work and require medical treatment or are provided with insurance against the costs of any necessary medical treatment overseas, the cost will be deductible for the employer and there's a specific exemption that applies to ensure that no benefit in kind arises.

The logic behind this exemption is that it's the travel away from home on business that has brought about the expense, and so the expense is essentially a travel cost (even though because of its nature there's a personal benefit).

The same principles could apply to the proprietor of an unincorporated business, but there's neither tax case law nor anything in the Taxman's internal guidance that deals with this point.

The Taxman does say that accommodation (which has a personal need of a not dissimilar nature) whilst travelling is a tax deductible cost for the proprietor of an unincorporated business, as it's a travelling expense. The same might very well be true of medical treatment needed overseas, or the costs of insuring against it.

Deduction 137. Legal and professional fees

Most legal and professional fees will be a tax deductible expense. There are two areas, though, where this will not be the case, where they relate:

- to the acquisition (successful or abortive) of a capital asset; or
- (wholly or in part) to the personal reputation of an individual in some way.

In the former case the costs will simply be non-deductible for both companies and unincorporated businesses, although the costs will follow the treatment of the asset concerned and might, therefore, qualify for capital allowances.

In the latter case, it will depend on whether there's a predominant business purpose for the proprietor of an unincorporated business. If there is, it will be deductible; if there isn't, there will be duality of purpose, meaning that it won't be deductible.

For an employee or director such a cost will be deductible for the employer, but there will be a benefit in kind and the costs will need to be apportioned between the personal and business purposes involved to determine the amount of the benefit.

CHAPTER 14

Publications and subscriptions

This chapter is all good news for those who incur costs on publications and subscriptions. These for the most part will be an allowable business expense for tax purposes, and this chapter highlights the major types of expenditure that will be allowable and what caveats apply.

Deduction 138. Books and maintaining libraries

Books used for the purposes of a business will be a tax deductible expense.

Where something like a professional library is first established and a large number of books are purchased, the Taxman may expect capital allowances to be claimed rather than a revenue expense deduction from taxable profits.

Thereafter, piecemeal additions and replacements should qualify for a revenue deduction.

Deduction 139. Trade and professional magazines

Similarly, any trade or professional magazines used for the purposes of the business will be a tax deductible expense (but some of the considerations in Deduction 140 may need to be taken into account), whether they are purchased on an ad hoc basis or by annual subscription.

Deduction 140. Newspapers and periodicals

Many businesses buy newspapers and non-trade periodicals to keep in reception areas for visitors and they may also be read by staff and proprietors.

If the predominant purpose of buying the newspapers and periodicals is for the business, the cost will be tax deductible and there won't be any benefit in kind on directors or employees.

If the business purpose is secondary, the cost won't be tax deductible in an unincorporated business. In a company there will be a benefit in kind on those who may use the magazines and periodicals, but the Taxman may be prepared to accept that this as an insignificant benefit that won't be taxable and doesn't need to be reported to him.

Deduction 141. Trade and professional subscriptions for businesses

Where a business pays for trade or professional subscriptions for the proprietor or for directors or employees, the expense will be deductible.

Deduction 142. Professional subscriptions for employees

Where an employee pays a subscription to a professional body (as well as to some unions and trade bodies) where membership of the body is relevant to their employment, it will be an expense that they can deduct from their taxable employment income.

If the employee reimburses such a subscription, it will be tax deductible for the employer and the employee will have both a taxable benefit and a corresponding expense deduction.

Deduction 143. Information services

Many employers subscribe to information services for marketing or credit control purposes (Dun and Bradstreet, FAME, Companies House Direct, for example) and the cost of these will be tax deductible, assuming that it has been incurred for the purposes of the business.

Deduction 144. HR/employment law services

Similarly, it's becoming increasingly common for employers to subscribe for a service through which they can obtain HR advice/assistance as and when they need it. This type of expense will be fully deductible from the business profits for tax purposes.

Deduction 145. Staff welfare services

Additionally, there are an increasing number of providers of subscription-based staff welfare services.

The idea of the service is that if the personal welfare needs of employees (when they're going through difficult patches in their personal lives, having financial troubles, facing stress or anxiety at work, for example) are taken care of, they will function better in the workplace.

There's a specific exemption in the tax legislation to prevent this sort of service from being a taxable benefit on the employees, making it even more attractive for employers to include it amongst their package of employee benefits.

Being employment-related, the costs of subscribing to such a service are fully tax deductible from the employer's business profits.

Deduction 146. Sky/Bloomberg, etc.

Just like newspapers and periodicals looked at in Deduction 140, a TV screen showing Sky News, Bloomberg or similar is now a feature of many a reception.

The same principles apply as for newspapers and periodicals. If the subscription expense is predominantly for a business purpose, any personal benefit for the proprietor or directors or employees will be disregarded. If the other way around, the expense will not be allowable for an unincorporated business and may give rise to benefits in kind in a company.

If the business is based at the proprietor's or owner-manager's home, and there's a business case for having a news screen in a reception area, it may be possible to make an apportionment of the costs, applying the principles for something like broadband, set out in Deductions 25 and 26 in Chapter 2.

The television itself will qualify for capital allowances.

Deduction 147. Gym memberships and similar expenses

Subscriptions, like gym or golf club membership, that provide personal benefits (as well as possibly business benefits) will not be deductible for an unincorporated business as they will not meet the condition of being wholly and exclusively for the purposes of the business.

For a company, the cost will be tax deductible for the business, but for the directors or employees concerned there will be a benefit in kind charge.

CHAPTER 15

Staff costs, pensions and employee share arrangements

This chapter focuses on the costs of employing staff (including family members) in the business and when they will be a deductible business expense. It also takes a look at tax relief on pensions and the tax effects of employee share arrangements.

Deduction 148. Wages and salaries

Salaries paid to employees and directors will be tax deductible. The wage or salary needs to have been paid within nine months of the end of the period to which it relates, otherwise it can't be deducted until the period in which it's paid.

Paid for this purpose means the earliest of when:

- a payment of or on account of the wage or salary is made; and
- the employee or director becomes entitled to the wage or salary.

Additionally, for directors a wage or salary will be paid at the earliest of the above events and:

- when any amount is credited in the company's books or accounts for the wage or salary
- the end of the period in question, where the amount has already been determined; and
- when the amount is determined, if it's done so after the end of the period in question.

These rules on payment do mean that, in most instances, payment of wages and salaries will take place within nine months of the end of the period to which it relates.

For company owner-managers, their overall remuneration must be paid wholly and exclusively for the purposes of the business. This will generally be the case, but if the overall remuneration is considered excessive, the excess over a reasonable remuneration will not be a tax deductible business expense.

For proprietors of unincorporated businesses, any wage or salary that they draw will not be deductible.

Deduction 149. Bonuses

In exactly the same way as regular wages and salaries need to be paid within nine months of the end of the period, so do any bonuses that might be paid. This nine-month rule is more likely to affect bonuses.

Many employers have formal or informal arrangements where profit or performance-related bonuses are paid to employees. At the end of the period the amount might not be known, but by the time the accounts are prepared, a reliable estimate may be able to be validly included in the accounts as a provision.

The bonus needs to be paid within nine months of the end of the period to avoid the tax relief being deferred.

Deduction 150. Wages and salaries for family members

Just as remuneration for company owner-managers shouldn't be excessive, the same applies to wages and salaries paid to other family members (spouses, partners and even children) employed in both incorporated and unincorporated businesses.

The wage or salary must be wholly and exclusively for the purposes of the business for tax relief to be obtained.

If the amount paid exceeds a reasonable remuneration, having regard to the duties performed, the excess will not be tax deductible.

Remember also that there are restrictions on the amount of work school age children can do and that under 13s can't be employed at all. Those over school age will be entitled to the National Minimum Wage.

Download Zone

For a **Spouse's Job Description**, visit **http://books.indicator.co.uk**. You'll find the access code on page 2 of this book.

Deduction 151. Individual pension contributions

Individuals can make pension contributions up to the greater of £3,600 or their relevant earnings. Their relevant earnings are the total taxable amounts for a tax year from:

- self-employments and partnerships
- employments and directorships (not including dividend payments)
- UK and EEA furnished holiday lettings profits; and
- patent income from inventions made by the individual.

Pension contributions will normally be paid net of basic rate tax, so to make a £3,600 pension contribution a payment of only £2,880 will need to be made to the pension company.

The individual will receive additional tax relief (at their highest marginal rate, less the basic rate tax relief given on the payment), if they pay tax above the basic rate.

There's an overall annual maximum that can be paid.

Deduction 152. Employer pension contributions

Pension contributions will be tax deductible for the employer, whilst the employee has no benefit in kind. This means the pension contributions are a popular salary sacrifice option.

For company owner-managers and their families, the wholly and exclusively rule applies and if their total remuneration package is excessive, the excess will not be tax deductible.

Additionally, there is a maximum amount of total individual and employer contributions that can be made each year. It's currently £50,000 but is being reduced to £40,000 in 2014/15. If the limit is exceeded, any unused amount from the previous three years (all years prior to 2014/15 had, or are deemed to have had, a £50,000 maximum) can be utilised.

If the annual allowance is exceeded, the excess is taxable by treating it as an amount of income for the individual, taxable at their marginal rates.

Deduction 153. Employee share arrangements - set-up costs

Employee share schemes are becoming increasingly popular, and the Taxman has established a number of approved scheme types. The costs of setting up the scheme will generally be deductible from the employer company's taxable business profits.

The costs of establishing an unapproved scheme, however, will usually not be tax deductible as they are capital in nature, but special consideration has been given to the approved schemes.

Deduction 154. Employee share arrangements - shares issued

Where shares are issued to employees and there's an employment tax charge on them (or there would be but for some exemption), the employer company will be entitled to tax relief on the value of shares issued.

Where shares are issued following the exercise of options provided to the employee some time previously, this tax deduction won't follow the accounting treatment. For accounting purposes, the value of the option is treated as an employment cost and then any additional value obtained is recognised when the option is exercised.

For tax purposes, tax relief is only given at the point at which the shares are finally issued.

Deduction 155. Other employee benefits

The costs of an employer providing any other benefits in kind that are taxable on an employee (or would be but for some exemption) will be tax deductible.

For company owner-managers and their family members the tax deduction will be restricted to the extent that the overall remuneration package is considered excessive.

CHAPTER 16

Finance costs and insurance

Most businesses incur finance costs of some sort and all businesses will need insurance of one description or another. This chapter looks at the various types of finance and insurance costs that could be incurred and how tax relief might be obtained for them.

Deduction 156. Overdraft interest

Any overdraft interest that a business incurs will normally be fully deductible.

For an unincorporated business, however, where the proprietor's drawings account (usually referred to as a current account, sometimes a capital account) is itself overdrawn, the Taxman may seek to restrict the allowable deduction accordingly.

Deduction 157. Credit card interest

Any interest incurred on a business credit card will be deductible.

Again, for an unincorporated business, to the extent that it relates to personal use, the interest will not be deductible. In an incorporated business the personal use of a business credit card will give rise to a benefit in kind, but will not prevent deduction of the credit card interest.

Deduction 158. Loan interest

Any loan interest that a business pays can be deducted in calculating the taxable profits of the business if it is incurred wholly and exclusively for the purposes of the business.

This will generally be the case if the loan was originally applied for a business purpose and there has been no effective change in the application of the loan (e.g. by selling a business asset that was purchased with a loan and applying the proceeds to some private purpose, or by appropriating such an asset to personal use).

Even if a loan in an unincorporated business is secured on a private asset, such as the proprietor's home, this will not, by itself, preclude deduction of the loan interest.

Deduction 159. Interest on loans to withdraw capital

One loan purpose that at first glance appears to be private in nature, but the Taxman expressly allows, is where the business takes out a loan to replace the proprietor's capital that is being withdrawn.

EXAMPLE

Malcolm had a property in which he lived and on which he had a £70,000 mortgage. A few years ago he got a job abroad and started to let the property. Its value at that time was £100,000, so Malcolm had effectively introduced a net £30,000 (£100,000 - £70,000) into his new property business.

Malcolm is now looking to purchase a property abroad to live in and needs additional funding of £25,000. Malcolm can raise additional borrowing of £25,000 in his property business and withdraw the funds from there to meet his personal funding requirement.

Since the additional borrowing within the business is being used to replace capital that Malcolm originally introduced into the business, but is now being withdrawn, interest on the additional £25,000 will be an allowable expense of the property business.

Deduction 160. Hire purchase interest and operating lease rentals

Any hire purchase interest or operating lease rentals that a business pays will usually be fully deductible, except in the following instances:

- where the asset concerned is used privately by a proprietor of an unincorporated business, the deduction will be restricted in proportion to the extent of the non-business use (in a company there will simply be a benefit in kind for the private use of the asset); and

- where the asset concerned is restricted, as referred to in Deduction 32 in Chapter 3.

Deduction 161. Incidental costs of obtaining finance

In addition to the interest on loans, any incidental costs of obtaining finance can also be deducted from the taxable business profits. This is if they are incurred wholly and exclusively for the purposes of the business, notwithstanding that they might otherwise be regarded as capital expenditure.

This will include valuation fees and arrangement fees. It will also cover any insurance that the business is obliged to take in order to secure the loan.

Deduction 162. General insurances

The general insurances of a business, such as professional indemnity, Public Liability and Employers' Liability will be fully deductible.

Any insurance that has both a business and a private element will usually not be deductible for an unincorporated business (and is likely to give rise in a benefit in kind in a company). See Deductions 25 and 26 in Chapter 2 (for household insurance where the home is used for business purposes) and Deduction 37 in Chapter 3 (regarding motor vehicle insurance).

Deductions 135 and 136 in Chapter 13 (regarding medical insurance) and deductions 163 and 164 below also need to be considered.

Deduction 163. Key person insurance

The cost of key person insurance will be allowable if it's incurred wholly and exclusively for the purposes of the business. This will be the case, where the beneficiary under the policy is the business (if lost business income is covered or if it will fund the salary of a replacement manager of requisite skill).

Where the premiums are allowable, any receipt under the policy will be taxable income of the business.

Where, however, the proprietor or a company owner-manager benefits from any receipt under the policy, the receipt will not be taxable business income, and the costs will not be deductible for an unincorporated business. For a company there are two possibilities where an owner-manager is the beneficiary; either:

- if they can only benefit in their capacity as a shareholder (because the benefit in some way protects the value of their shares, for example), the expense will not be tax deductible and there may be a deemed dividend on the amount; or
- if they benefit as a private individual, it's likely to be linked to their directorship, meaning that the cost will be tax deductible for the company, but the director will have a benefit in kind.

Deduction 164. Income/profit protection insurance

Similarly, the costs of any other policy, the purpose of which is to protect the business from lost income, will be tax deductible.

Care needs to be taken to ensure that the policy is for the purpose of protecting the business, rather than an individual, from lost income, particularly in an unincorporated business. Some policies are for the purpose of protecting the individual from the effects of lost income within the business if they are unable to work.

Deduction 165. Professional indemnity insurance

Where an employee or director needs, or is required, to maintain their own professional indemnity insurance (or similar), that will be an expense that they can deduct from their taxable employment income (including any reimbursement by the employer).

CHAPTER 17

Provision of finance

Businesses raise finance in a number of ways and this chapter looks at how individuals can obtain tax relief on things they may do personally that relate to the raising of finance by businesses, which might be, but not necessarily, the individual's own business.

Deduction 166. Tax relief on interest paid

Where an individual takes out a loan, they can claim a tax deduction against their personal income tax bill if it was taken out for one of the following purposes:

- to buy plant and machinery used in a partnership of which the individual is a member or in the individual's employment (relief on interest is only available for a period of three years in either case)

- to buy shares in or lend money to either a close company (other than a close investment holding company) or an employee-controlled company

- to invest in a partnership of which the individual is (when the interest is paid) a member.

In each case, there are a number of conditions imposed in order to prevent abuse, and income tax relief on interest on a loan to buy shares can't be claimed if the individual also wants income tax relief under EIS or SEIS.

EXAMPLE

Anthony took out a loan of £100,000 on March 31 2013 to contribute capital to a professional partnership of which he has now become a partner, having been an employee of the partnership up until March 31 2013.

The loan is secured on his home on a fixed rate deal for five years at 3.5% and he will pay interest of £3,500 annually.

He can deduct the £3,500 from his taxable income each year, before calculating his tax liability, for as long as he remains a partner, or until the loan is repaid, provided none of the capital is repaid to him.

Deduction 167. EIS income tax relief

Where an individual subscribes for shares that qualify under the Enterprise Investment Scheme (EIS), tax relief at 30% on up to £1 million of investment can be deducted from the individual's income tax liability (but not so as to make it negative).

Investments of up to the current tax year's £1 million maximum can be treated as paid in the previous tax year and relief claimed in that year if preferred. Any amount so treated will reduce the current year's maximum.

The shares need to be held for at least three years. If they're sold, or for any reason the shares or the company cease to qualify under EIS, the income tax relief will be withdrawn. After three years, if the income tax relief hasn't been withdrawn, the shares will be exempt from Capital Gains Tax (CGT).

These reliefs are, however, are only available to people who aren't connected with the company, as would be the case for an owner-manager.

EXAMPLE

Clive invested £250,000 in shares in an EIS company on February 28 2013. His 2012/13 income tax liability before relief for the EIS investment is £40,000 and was a similar amount in 2011/12.

The maximum relief available on the investment is £75,000 (£250,000 x 30%) which exceeds his income tax liability, so that £35,000 of the available tax relief will waste in 2012/13.

However, if Clive elects to treat at least £116,667 (tax relief £35,000) as having been invested in 2011/12, he will be able to obtain relief for the whole investment across the two years.

Deduction 168. SEIS income tax relief

The Seed Enterprise Investment Scheme (SEIS) works in almost exactly the same way as EIS, and investments made by an individual of up to £50,000 in a tax year in shares that qualify under SEIS are eligible for tax relief at 50% of the amount invested. The tax relief is set against the individual's income tax liability of the tax year of investment (but not so as to make it negative).

Investment amounts can be treated as paid in the previous year in the same way as EIS and the shares will also be exempt if they aren't sold (or the income tax relief is otherwise withdrawn) within three years.

Again, the reliefs aren't available to anyone connected with the company, such as an owner-manager.

Deduction 169. VCT income tax relief

Companies are also able to raise capital through Venture Capital Trusts (VCTs) and individuals are able to invest in the VCTs themselves. Amounts so invested of up to £200,000 in any tax year are eligible for income tax relief at 30% of the amount invested.

Again, the relief is set against the individual's income tax liability (but can't turn it negative). The relief will be withdrawn if the shares are sold within a period of five years following investment.

Whenever the VCT shares are sold, they will be exempt from CGT.

Deduction 170. EIS Capital Gains Tax deferral relief

Anybody who subscribes for EIS shares (including the company owner-manager) can use them to defer any capital gains that arise in the same tax year as the investment. To the extent that the amount of the gain has been invested in the EIS shares it won't become chargeable to tax until the EIS shares are sold.

EXAMPLE

Maria has recently sold a house that she has been letting. She has made a £50,000 gain. If she now subscribes for £50,000 of shares, she will potentially receive £25,000 of income tax relief.

She can also use the shares to defer the gain on the house and it won't become chargeable to CGT until she sells the shares.

Download Zone

For a **CGT EIS Deferral Relief Claim**. visit **http://books.indicator.co.uk**. You'll find the access code on page 2 of this book.

CHAPTER 18

Starting up in business

It's often the case that expenses are incurred before trade actually commences. This chapter deals with how relief can be obtained for such expenditure.

Deduction 171. Capital expenditure incurred before the business commences

Where expenditure incurred before the business is capital in nature (it brings an asset into existence that will provide enduring benefits to the business) it may qualify for capital allowances.

If the expenditure would qualify for capital allowances. then it will be treated as if it was actually incurred on the first day of the business, meaning that the relevant capital allowances can still be claimed.

EXAMPLE

Jeremy has bought a van to use in the business that he will be starting on June 1 2013. For capital allowances purposes, Jeremy will be treated as if he purchased the van on June 1 2013 when the business starts.

Deduction 172. Revenue expenditure incurred before the business commences

Similarly, for revenue expenditure (expenditure that isn't capital as defined above) will be treated as having been incurred on the first day of business and will be deductible if it's incurred wholly and exclusively for the purposes of the business.

So any expenditure that is referred to as being deductible from business profits, will be deductible on day one if it happens to be incurred before the business commences.

The Taxman will generally accept that where an owner-manager of an incorporated business incurs expenditure in relation to the company's intended business they do so as agent, even if the company hasn't been incorporated when the expenditure is incurred. However, costs in relation to incorporation of a company are regarded as non-allowable capital expenditure.

EXAMPLE

Destrier Ltd was incorporated on May 1 2013 and commenced trading on June 1 2013. Prior to incorporation the directors had spent £3,000 on the company's website.

The website costs don't meet the criteria to be regarded as capital expenditure and so would be deductible revenue expenditure if incurred by the company on or after June 1 2013.

Whilst the directors incurred the costs prior to either formation of the company or beginning to trade, they will be treated as having incurred the expenditure as the company's agent, and the company will be treated as if it incurred the expenditure on June 1 2013.

This means that the £3,000 can be deducted from the company's taxable profits for its first period of trading.

Deduction 173. Input VAT incurred before VAT registration

Where input VAT has been incurred prior to VAT registration (which may happen after the business has commenced, then the business may be able to recover that VAT.

Input VAT can be recovered on supplies of:

- services received up to six months prior to registration

- goods received up to four months prior to registration, provided the goods are still held at registration.

EXAMPLE

Nikabrik Ltd registered for VAT on April 1 2013. It had previously incurred the following amounts of VAT:

- £2,000 on consultancy fees of £10,000 invoiced on November 11 2012

- £3,000 on consultancy fees of £10,000 invoiced on February 11 2013; and

- £4,000 on computer equipment costing £20,000 purchased on January 6 2013.

Because the first consultancy fees were supplied more than six month prior to registration, the input VAT can't be recovered.

However, assuming that the company still has the computer equipment, it will be able to recover the other £7,000 of input VAT on its first VAT return.

CHAPTER 19

Losses

Where the expenses that a business can deduct from its profits exceed the income so that a loss arises, there are a number of ways that the loss might be used depending on the type of business and whether it is unincorporated or operated through a company.

This chapter looks at the various ways that a deduction might be obtained for such a loss, but where a company carries out research and development, the deductions in Chapter 6 should also be considered.

Deduction 174. Companies - trading losses carried forward

Where a company incurs a trading loss, then unless one of the other claims mentioned in this chapter is made, the loss will be carried forward automatically and set against the next available profits of the same trade.

Deduction 175. Individuals - trading losses carried forward

Similarly, trading losses for individuals will, by default, be carried forward and set against the first available profits of the same trade, even if that might cause the individual's personal allowance to be wasted.

Deduction 176. Individuals - trading losses for Class 4 NI purposes

For the purposes of Class 4 NI, whatever a self-employed individual does with their trading loss, it will be carried forward and set against the next available trading profits.

EXAMPLE

Brian has made a loss of £10,000 in his first year of trading to March 31 2013. In the following year to March 31 2014 he expects to make a profit of £18,000.

By default, the 2012/13 loss of £10,000 will be carried forward and set against the £15,000 profit in 2013/14, leaving £8,000 taxable. If Brian has no other income this amount will be covered by his personal allowance, but £2,000 of his 2013/14 personal allowance will waste.

Even if Brian elects to do something different with the loss for tax purposes, his profit in 2013/14 for the purposes of Class 4 NI will be £8,000.

Deduction 177. Companies - trading losses carried sideways

An alternative for companies is to set their trading loss against any other profits or gains (including capital gains) the company may have in the same accounting period.

Deduction 178. Individuals - trading losses carried sideways

Individuals are also able to set their trading loss for a tax year against their other taxable income of the same tax year. From the tax year 2013/14 the maximum amount that can be set off in any one year is £50,000.

Additionally, in certain circumstances, relief for a trading loss arising from a sole-trade may be restricted to £25,000 in any one year, and relief for a loss from a partnership will be restricted in total to the amount of capital contribution that the individual has made to the partnership.

The circumstances are where the individual is a member of a limited liability partnership or a limited partner of a limited partnership, from which the loss arises, or devotes less than ten hours per week on average to the business.

Using the loss in this way may cause the individual's personal allowance to waste. The set-off is only restricted by the amount of available income.

Deduction 179. Companies - trading losses carried back

Once a company's trading loss has been fully utilised against any other profits or gains of the same period under Deduction 177, any remaining balance can be carried back and set against Corporation Tax (CT) accounting periods falling wholly or partly in the preceding twelve months.

To the extent that a CT accounting period doesn't fall wholly within the twelve months preceding the loss-making period, the loss can only be set against an appropriate proportion of the period's profits that relate to the part that does fall within the twelve-month period.

EXAMPLE

Restimar Ltd has a trading loss in its twelve-month accounting period to June 30 2013 of £8,000 and other taxable income and gains of £2,000.

The previous accounting periods were for the four months to June 30 2012 when total profits were £1,000 and for the twelve months to February 29 2012 when total profits were £4,500.

Restimar must first set the £8,000 loss against the other income and gains of the same period, using £2,000. The remaining £6,000 can be carried back and used against the £1,000 profits of the four-month period to June 30 2012, leaving £5,000.

In the twelve-month period to February 29 2012, only the last eight moths fall in the twelve months preceding the period of the loss, so the maximum amount of profits against which losses can be set is £3,000 (£4,500 x 8/12ths).

£4,500 of the remaining £5,000 of losses can be set off in the period to February 29 2012 (profits of just £1,500 will now be taxable for that period), and the remaining £500 of trading losses will have to be carried forward.

Deduction 180. Individuals - trading losses carried back

As an alternative or in addition to Deduction 178, an individual can set their trading loss for a tax year against their total income of the previous year. Once again, the maximum amount that can be set off from 2013/14 onwards is £50,000 and the restriction for certain losses referred to in Deduction 178 also applies.

Again, setting the loss off in this way is only restricted to the amount of available income and so may cause the individual's personal allowance to waste.

Deduction 181. Individuals - trading losses set against capital gains

To the extent that an individual's trading loss of a tax year can't be used under Deductions 178 or 180 due to there being insufficient other income in the current and preceding tax years, the loss can also be set against any capital gains that the individual may have in the same tax year.

This relief isn't subject to the £50,000 restriction referred to in Deduction 178, but is subject to the restriction that applies to certain losses referred to in Deduction 178.

EXAMPLE

Sheila has incurred a trading loss for 2012/13 of £70,000. She has other taxable income in 2012/13 of £20,000, as well as capital gains of £18,000, and had total taxable income in 2011/12 of £25,000.

Sheila can set £20,000 of her loss against her 2012/13 income, but her personal allowance of £8,105 will then be wasted.

As an alternative, or in addition, to that she can set £25,000 of the loss against her 2011/12 income, but her personal allowance of £7,475 for that year will be wasted.

If she makes both of these claims, she can also set £18,000 of the loss against her 2012/13 capital gains (wasting her annual exemption of £10,600) if she wishes.

If she makes all three claims, £7,000 of losses (£70,000 - £20,000 - £25,000 - £18,000) will be carried forward and set against the next available profits of the trade.

Deduction 182. Individuals - trading losses in the early years of trading

Another alternative that an individual has for any trading losses that arise in their first four tax years of trading is to set the trade loss against their total income of the three tax years preceding the loss, earliest year first. The maximum amount that can be set off in any tax year from 2013/14 onwards is £50,000.

Once again, setting losses off in this way is only restricted to the amount of available income and so may cause wastage of the individual's personal allowance.

EXAMPLE

If Sheila's loss in the above example had been incurred in the second year of trading and she had taxable income in 2009/10 and 2010/11 of £40,000 and £35,000, respectively, this would have been a better claim for her.

She could have carried the £70,000 loss back against the preceding three years' taxable incomes, earliest first.

£40,000 would be first set against the income of 2009/10, wasting that year's personal allowance. The remaining £30,000 would be set against the 2010/11 income of £35,000, leaving £5,000 taxable, which would be covered by Sheila's personal allowance for that year.

Deduction 183. Company - terminal trading losses

When a company an overall trading loss in its final year of trading, it can set the loss against its total profits and gains of the current year and then carry that loss back against its total profits and gains of the previous three years, starting with the latest year.

EXAMPLE

Zardeenah Ltd has made a loss in its final four-month period of trading to April 30 2013 of £50,000, having made a trading loss in the year ended December 31 2012 of £120,000. It has no other income in either of these periods.

It had total taxable income in the years ended December 31 2010 and 2011 of £90,000 and £50,000, respectively.

Its terminal loss must first be calculated for the twelve months to April 30 2013. This is £130,000 (£50,000 for the four months to April 30 2013 plus 8/12ths of the £120,000 for the year to December 3 2012).

This can be set against any income from accounting periods falling in the three years prior to the terminal period, latest first. This includes any period that ends after May 1 2010.

£50,000 is first set against the profits from the year ended December 31 2011 (there being no profits in 2012), leaving £80,000.

In the year ended December 31 2010, only the last eight months fall in the three-year period preceding the terminal twelve-month period, so the terminal loss can only be set against up to £60,000 (£90,000 x 8/12ths) of profits.

That means £20,000 of the remaining £80,000 of terminal loss can't be relieved.

Deduction 184. Individuals - terminal trading losses

Similarly, when an individual makes an overall trading loss in their final year of trading, they can also carry that loss back against its previous three years' profits from the same trade, latest year first.

EXAMPLE

Michael has a loss in his final year of trading to March 31 2013 of £25,000. He had profits in the previous three years to March 31 2010, 2011 and 2012 of £9,000, £10,000 and £11,000.

The loss will be carried back and set against the previous three years' trading profits, latest first; £11,000 in the year to March 31 2012, then £10,000 in the year to March 31 2011.

The remaining £4,000 of the loss will be set against the £9,000 of trading profit in the year to March 31 2010, leaving £5,000 of trading profit taxable in 2009/10. Any other income in any of the years will remain taxable.

Deduction 185. Companies - property business losses

Where a company carries on any property business (aggregating all rental activity) and makes a loss, that loss is automatically set against the total profits and gains of that year, and then carried forward and treated as if it's a property business loss arising in the following year (automatically set against that year's total profits and gains and then carried forward, etc.).

EXAMPLE

Reepicheep Ltd has a loss from its property business of £10,000 in the year ended May 31 2013, and other income of £4,000. The loss will first be set against the £4,000 income from the same year, and the remaining £6,000 will be carried forward and treated as a loss arising in the next period.

If in the next year to May 31 2014 Reepicheep has total income of £5,000, this will be covered by £5,000 of the £6,000 property loss that has been carried forward and treated as arising in that period.

The remaining £1,000 of loss will then be carried forward and treated as a loss arising in the next period.

Deduction 186. Individuals - furnished holiday letting losses

Up until 2010/11 losses from UK furnished holiday lettings for individuals were treated as trades for the purposes of all loss reliefs with some very slight modification.

From 2011/12 losses from an individual's UK and EEA furnished holiday lettings can only be carried forward and set against future profits of the appropriate overall separate UK and EEA furnished holiday lettings business - in a similar way for losses from UK and overseas property businesses described in Deduction 188.

Furnished holiday lettings outside the EEA are treated as any other property business for individuals.

Deduction 187. Individuals - property business losses representing capital allowances

To the extent that an individual's property business loss (from either their UK or overseas property business) comprises capital allowances, that amount can be set against the individual's total income of either or both of the current and subsequent tax years.

Using the loss in this way may cause the individual's personal allowance to waste. The set-off is only restricted by the amount of available income.

Deduction 188. Individuals - other property business losses

For any property losses that aren't from UK or EEA furnished holiday letting and which aren't relieved under Deduction 187, the loss can only be carried forward and set against the appropriate UK or overseas property business.

Apart from UK and EEA furnished holiday lettings, all of an individual's UK property rental activities are aggregated into an overall UK property rental business and all their overseas rental activities are similarly treated.

Any losses of the UK rental property business can't be set against profits from the overseas rental business or vice versa, except where relief is obtained against the individual's total income using Deduction 187.

Deduction 189. Companies - non-trade loan relationship deficits

The interest a company pays and receives, as well as foreign exchange gains and losses and any other accounting debits and credits relating to loans and similar financial instruments fall under what is called the loan relationships legislation.

Any amounts that don't relate to trading activity are regarded as non-trade loan relationship debits and credits. To the extent that the non-trade credits exceed the non-trade debits, the surplus is taxable as part of the company's total taxable profits.

Where, however, debits exceed credits there is a non-trade loan relationship deficit, which (subject to Deduction 190) can be relieved in one of three ways:

- by default, by being carried forward and set against non-trade income, gains (including capital gains) and surpluses of subsequent accounting periods
- by set-off against the company's total income and gains of the same accounting period
- by set-off against the company's total income and gains of Corporation Tax accounting periods ending in the preceding twelve months (in a similar way to Deduction 179).

EXAMPLE

In its twelve-month accounting period ended February 28 2012 Darrin Ltd has received interest on an investment of £4,000 and has paid loan interest on a non-trade loan of £10,000. It therefore has a non-trade loan relationship deficit of £6,000.

It has other taxable income in the year of £3,000 and had taxable income in the previous year of £1,000. It is anticipating a capital gain in the following year of £9,000.

By default, the deficit will be carried forward and set against the gain in the subsequent period.

However, Darrin can set £3,000 of the deficit against its current taxable income and carry £1,000 back against the previous year's taxable income. £2,000 will then be carried forward and can be set against the later capital gain.

Deduction 190. Companies - group relief for losses

Where two, or more, companies are (directly or indirectly) at least 75% owned by a third company or where one company owns the other(s) in that way, they will be members of a group for Corporation Tax group relief purposes, allowing certain losses and deficits to be passed between them.

A company that is a member of such a group can surrender any trade losses, property business losses or non-trade deficits that arose in the current accounting period to another member of the group which can then relieve them against its total profits and gains in their current accounting period.

For property business losses, it's only the actual loss that arose in the period that can be surrendered and not any amount that is deemed to have arisen in the current period but has, in fact, been brought forward from an earlier accounting period.

The maximum amount that can be surrendered is the lesser of the amount of the surrendering company's loss and the amount of the recipient company's total taxable profits and gains.

Where the two companies' accounting periods don't coincide or they weren't members of the same group for the whole period, the maximum amount is that calculated in this way for the common period.

EXAMPLE

Olvin Ltd and Rilian Ltd both have twelve-month accounting periods ended December 31 2012. They have been members of a group since May 1 2012 (the last eight months of the period). Olvin has a property business loss for the period of £9,000 and Rilian has profits of £7,500 for the period.

The maximum amount of the loss that Olvin can surrender is £6.000 (£9,000 x 8/12ths) and the maximum amount that Rilian can receive is £5,000 (7,500 x 8/12ths). Olvin can, therefore, surrender £5,000 of its £9,000 loss to Rilian, leaving Rilian with £3,500 of taxable profits,

Being a property business loss the remaining £4,000 of Olvin's loss can only be set against any other profits it may have in the current period, or carried forward and treated as a property business loss arising to Olvin in the subsequent period (but not then available for group relief).

Had it been a trading loss. Olvin would also have been able to carry any residual loss (after setting against current income) back to the previous period if it had taxable income in that period.

Deduction 191. Companies - capital losses

A company's capital gains and losses for an accounting period are aggregated. If there's an overall gain, it's taxable with the company's other income of the accounting period.

If there's an overall capital loss, it can be carried forward and set against any overall capital gains of a future accounting period, but can't be relieved in any other way.

EXAMPLE

Ketterley Ltd has sold three assets in its accounting period ended December 31 2009 and made capital gains on two of them of £4,000 and £2,000, plus has made a capital loss on the third of £9.000. It therefore had an overall capital loss for the year of £3.000.

Now in its accounting period ended December 31 2012 it has sold two assets. making a capital loss of £2.000 on one and a capital gain of £9.000 on the other. Overall, it has a capital gain of £7.000.

The £3,000 brought forward loss can be set against the £7,000 gain and only capital gains of £5,000 will be taxable.

Download Zone

For a **Trading Loss Relief Claim**, visit **http://books.indicator.co.uk**. You'll find the access code on page 2 of this book.

Deduction 192. Individuals - capital losses on shares in unquoted trading companies

For individuals, any capital loss arising on shares in unquoted trading companies (which might arise on a negligible value claim) can either be used like any other capital loss, or it can be set against the individual's total income of either or both of the tax year in which the loss arose or the preceding tax year.

This applies in particular to EIS and SEIS shares. Where the shares were the subject of a claim to income tax relief under EIS or SEIS, the amount of the loss is reduced by the amount of income tax that was originally claimed (and hasn't been withdrawn).

EXAMPLE

Helen subscribed for some EIS shares a number of years ago for £10,000 on which she received income tax relief of £3,000. The shares are now worthless and Helen has made a negligible value claim, realising a capital loss of £7,000 (£10,000).

She can claim a deduction from her current income for this £7,000 loss.

Deduction 193. Individuals - other capital losses

Apart from losses on shares in unquoted trading companies where Deduction 192 is claimed, all of an individual's capital gains and losses for a tax year are aggregated. Any overall gain is taxed (subject to deduction of the annual exemption).

Any overall loss is carried forward and set against any capital gains of future tax years, but only to the extent that those gains aren't covered by that year's annual exemption.

Deduction 194. Negligible value claims

Where a company or an individual has an asset (any gain on which would be a taxable capital gain) which has become of negligible value, it can make a claim to treat the asset as if it's then sold and reacquired at its then (negligible) value in order to realise a capital loss to set against the company's or individual's other capital gains, or, in the case of shares in an unquoted trading company, held by an individual against income.

The claim can be backdated up to two years prior to the time of the claim if the asset was also of negligible value at that time.

Download Zone

For a **Negligible Value Claim**, visit **http://books.indicator.co.uk**. You'll find the access code on page 2 of this book.

CHAPTER 20

And finally...

This final chapter looks at a few other points that haven't fitted in neatly elsewhere.

Deduction 195. Gift Aid for individuals

Where an individual makes a gift to charity, they are able to give a declaration to the charity that they are a taxpayer. This enables the charity to treat the gift as having been made after deduction of basic rate tax by the individual, which it can then reclaim from the Taxman.

If the individual pays tax at a higher rate, they can then obtain further tax relief on the gift grossed up for basic rate tax on the difference between their highest marginal rate and the basic rate.

EXAMPLE

Lorna has recently donated £80 to a small local charity and, being a higher rate taxpayer, has made a Gift Aid declaration.

The charity can treat the gift as being a gross £100 from which Lorna has deducted basic rate tax at 20%, and it can recover that £20 from the Taxman.

Lorna can also receive an additional £20 tax relief (40% - 20%) on the gross £100 gift, having obtained basic rate relief when she made the gift by paying only £80.

Deduction 196. Gift Aid for companies

Gift Aid is also available to companies, but works slightly differently, because there is no deemed tax deduction. The amount gifted to a charity by a company can simply be deducted from its taxable profits (but can't create a loss).

Deduction 197. Community Investment Tax Relief

Investments designed to provide finance to businesses located in disadvantaged areas or to serve members of disadvantaged groups can attract tax relief. This is given as a tax reduction at 5% of the amount invested.

Deduction 198. Class 2 NI small earning exception

All self-employed people (aged over 16 and below state retirement age) are required to pay flat rate Class 2 NI contributions.

However, if an individual expects their profit from their self-employment (or partnership) to be less than a certain threshold, they can apply for what's called the small earnings exception meaning that they won't have to pay these contributions.

For 2013/14 this threshold is £5.725.

Deduction 199. Class 2 and 4 NI contribution deferment

Additionally, the self-employed (aged over 16 and below state retirement age) will pay Class 4 NI contributions as a percentage of their taxable business profits (9% between £7,755 and £41,450 and 2% above £41,450 for 2013/14).

Where, however, they also have earnings from employment which exceed £41,450 in 2013/14, they can apply to defer their Class 2 and Class 4 NI contributions.

They will then only have to pay Class 4 NI on their business profits above £7,755 at 2%.

CHAPTER 21

Documents

BUSINESS MILEAGE RECORD

Name ....   Car registration ....

Business journeys during the month of ....   Year ....

Date	From	To	Reason	Miles	Claim (£)

Notes

The HMRC expects the Company to keep a record of the amounts paid for business mileage in your company car and the business journeys they are for. To facilitate this you are required to fill out a monthly mileage record in addition to your normal expense claim for business miles travelled at the "advisory fuel rates for company cars".

The rates are reviewed quarterly.

CALCULATION OF GOODWILL PRO FORMA

Name:

T/A:

Calculation of goodwill as at:

	£	£

Profit history (sole trader or partnership)

Year-ended:		0
Year-ended:		0
Year-ended:		0
		0

Average annual profit (last three years) — 0

Profit projection (Company)

Estimated projected maintainable profits — 0

Yield on capital investment

Net assets (excluding cash)	0	
Yield (say base rate + 1.25%)	0%	0

Calculation of super profits

Estimated projected maintainable profits	0
Less: Yield on capital investment	0
Less: Deemed manager's salary	0
Super profit	0

Goodwill calculation

Assume 2.5 multiplier	0
Less: Personal element (say 20%)	0
Goodwill valuation agreed	0

Note:

We believe the following factors create a conservative valuation:

1. Maintainable profits
2. Manager's salary
3. Multiplier
4. Personal goodwill

Price adjuster clause

Should the parties become aware that a fair market price is different from this figure, the price shall be adjusted accordingly.

CAPITAL ALLOWANCES CHECKLIST

Capital allowances can only be claimed on plant and machinery and not on buildings. However, the legislation specifies those assets that, while falling under the definition of buildings, will qualify as plant. These items are listed separately under their relevant section.

Asset description	Date acquired	Original cost (£)	Capital allowances [already claimed] (£)	Sale value (£)
Electrical systems (specific to trade):				
Wiring to fixed plant				
Switchgear				
Emergency lighting				
Specialised lighting (e.g. window display)				
Other:				
Space and water heating systems				
Hot water system				
Air conditioning (including any associated suspended ceiling or floor)				
Air purification system				
Manufacturing or processing equipment (list):				
Storage equipment (list):				

Asset description	Date acquired	Original cost (£)	Capital allowances [already claimed] (£)	Sale value (£)
Cold room				
Display equipment (list):				
White goods:				
Cooker				
Washing machine				
Dishwasher				
Refrigerator				
Other:				
Sanitary fittings:				
Washbasins				
Sinks				

Asset description	Date acquired	Original cost (£)	Capital allowances [already claimed] (£)	Sale value (£)
Baths				
Showers				
Other:				
Networking systems:				
Computer network system (including wiring)				
Telephone network system (including wiring)				
Walkways:				
Lifts				
Hoists				
Escalators				

Documents

Asset description	Date acquired	Original cost (£)	Capital allowances [already claimed] (£)	Sale value (£)
Moving walkways				
Fire and security equipment:				
CCTV				
Sound insulation				
Fire alarm system				
Fire extinguishers				
Sprinkler system				
Mechanical door closers				
Other fire-fighting equipment				
Burglar alarm system				
Safe				

Asset description	Date acquired	Original cost (£)	Capital allowances [already claimed] (£)	Sale value (£)
Other:				
Fixtures and fittings:				
Moveable partitioning				
Carpets				
Removable floor coverings				
Blinds				
Curtains				
Mezzanine floor				
Trade and information signs				
Any other machinery not listed above:				
TOTAL DISPOSAL VALUE				

CAPITAL ALLOWANCES ELECTION

Notification of an Election to use an alternative apportionment in accordance with s.198 **Capital Allowances Act 2001**, between .... *(insert name of seller)* and .... *(insert name of buyer)*.

Property address:..

Interest (freehold/leasehold): ....

Seller's name and address:..

Tax district and reference:...

Buyer's name and address: ....

Tax district and reference:............. ....

Date of completion of sale: ....

Amount apportioned to machinery and plant fixtures (£):...
(see attached for details)

Sale price (£): ....

The seller and the buyer hereby jointly elect, pursuant to the provisions of s.198 Capital Allowances Act 2001, that the amount of the sale price to be treated as capital expenditure on plant and machinery incurred by the buyer on the provision of the fixtures is .... *(insert amount as above)*. A list of the fixtures is given on the next page.

Signed: ....

Name of Seller: ....

Date: ....

Signed: ....

Name of Buyer: ....

Date: ....

Example:

Schedule of Plant and Machinery to included in s.198 Election

.... *(insert address)*

Item	Apportioned Amount
Ventilation	£4,500.00
Blinds	£1,500.00
Total	**£6,000.00**

CLAUSES FOR CONTRACT

1. Have any of the Fixtures included in the transaction been included in an election either under s.198 or s.199 Capital Allowances Act 2001 (previously s.59B of the Capital Allowances Act 1990)? If so, please provide a copy of such election notice(s).

2. If requested by us, will you enter into an agreement with us to make an election under s.198 or s.199 of the Capital Allowances Act 2001?

CGT EIS DEFERRAL RELIEF CLAIM

HM Revenue & Customs

.... *(insert tax office address)*
....
....
....
....

.... *(insert date)*

Dear Sir

.... **(insert your tax reference)**

Claim For Capital Gains EIS Deferral Relief

Re: Disposal of .... *(insert details of the disposal)* dated .... *(insert date of disposal)*

In accordance with Sch 5B of the Taxation of Chargeable Gains Act 1992, I wish to defer the capital gain of .... *(insert amount of gain)* on my disposal of the above mentioned assets as I have invested the proceeds into:

.... *(insert number and details of EIS shares acquired)* on ....*(insert date of purchase of EIS shares).*

We attach a computation of the capital gain to be deferred and the *EIS3* or EIS5** certificate.

Yours faithfully

....

(* The company in which the investment is made must supply you with the EIS3 certificate showing the amount of your investment elgible for CGT deferral relief. If you invested through a fund or investment manager they wi!l issue an EIS5 instead.)

ELECTION FOR RENT-A-ROOM RELIEF NOT TO APPLY

HMRC

.... *(insert address)*

....

....

....

.... *(insert date)*

Dear Sirs

Rent-a-room

.... ***(insert your name)***

.... ***(insert your ten-digit tax reference)***

In accordance with s.799 of the Income Tax Trading and Other Income Act 2005 I elect that for the year ………….. *(insert the tax year for which you want the election to apply)* rent-a-room relief shall not apply to the income I received from letting ……………………… *(insert the address of the property).*

[*(Or where you wish to withdraw a previous election)*

In accordance with s.799 of the Income Tax Trading and Other Income Act 2005 I hereby withdraw the election previously made that for the year ………….. *(insert the tax year for which you want the election to apply)* rent-a-room relief shall not apply to the income I received from letting …………………………………. *(insert the address of the property).*]

Yours faithfully

…………………………………. *(insert signature)*

HOMEWORKERS' EXPENSES POLICY

Provision of equipment

The Company will supply you with the necessary equipment that may reasonably be required to enable the contract to be performed from home. This may include some of the following:

- telephone
- fax machine
- laptop/desktop computer
- computer software/licences
- printer
- photocopier
- desk and chair
- filing cabinet(s)
- desk stationery
- writing materials.

An inventory will be kept as a means of recording the equipment supplied and you will be required to sign for the receipt of any equipment provided.

The equipment shall at all times remain the property of the Company, not be used for private purposes and be returned by you when you cease working from home. All equipment supplied by the Company will be covered under the Company's insurance policy.

Travel

You will be recorded as having your home as your permanent place of work. Therefore travel between your home and the Company's premises, or any other location visited on behalf of the Company, is regarded as business travel and will be reimbursed under the normal expenses policy rules.

Telephone

See the separate provision of home telephone policy.

Additional home expenses

The additional costs of such things as heating and lighting, which arise due to you working from home will be reimbursed at a flat rate of £4 per week.

INCIDENTAL OVERNIGHT EXPENSES POLICY

Personal incidental expenses, for example, personal telephone calls, newspapers, laundry etc., incurred whilst staying away overnight on Company business, must be excluded from the accommodation costs. They should be identified separately on the invoice by the hotel, or if this is not possible, highlighted by the claimant and excluded on the expenses claim. The Company will not reimburse invoices that do not show any personal expense items separately. The employee will be responsible for these costs.

The maximum amount that can be claimed per night on personal incidental expenses is equivalent to HMRC's tax-free limits which are currently:

Staying away in the United Kingdom	£5.00 (inclusive of VAT)
Staying away overseas	£10.00 (inclusive of VAT)

The employee must reimburse the Company for any amounts in excess of these tax-free limits by July 6, following the tax year in which the overpayment occurred.

LICENCE AGREEMENT

This agreement is made on .... *(insert date)* between

(1) .... *(insert company name)* (the "Company") and

(2) .... *(insert property owner's name)* (the "Property Owners")

(3) .... *(insert property owner's name)* (the "Property Owners")

It is agreed that

1. The Property Owners jointly own .... *(insert address of the property)* (the "Property").

2. The Property includes accommodation and contains furniture ("the Home Office") which is available for use by the Company and which it is envisaged shall be used by the Company from time to time.

3. It is agreed that in consideration for its use of the Home Office (between the hours of 9am and 5pm), the Company shall reimburse to the Property Owners such proportion of any expenses they incur in providing it as is fairly attributable to the use of the Home Office by the Company including (but without limitation) provision of broadband facilities, a proportion of mortgage interest, insurance, heating and lighting costs, maintenance and repair. The proportion is to be agreed between the parties from time to time having regard to the actual use made by the Company of the Home Office.

Signed on behalf of the Company ....

Name (in capitals) ....

Position...

Signed by the Property Owners (1) ....

Signed by the Property Owners (2) ....

Date ....

LUMP SUM CONTRIBUTION AGREEMENT

Agreement concerning a capital contribution towards the purchase of company car registration ……………..... *(insert registration number)* (the "Car") to be provided by ……………...... *(insert company name)* (the "Company") for private use by ………………………………... *(insert name)* (the "Director/Employee").

The Employee agrees to make a capital contribution of ….. *(insert figure*)* towards the purchase of the Car, to be paid by the employee within 30 days of the Car being purchased by the Company.

Upon sale of the Car, the Employee will be entitled to a refund of said capital contribution, but only after the Employee's share of depreciation in market value since purchase has been taken into account.

Agreement
As a condition of the Car being available, I agree to make the payment referred to above and accept a deduction for depreciation from any refund due to me when the Car is sold.

Signed...

Date ....

* *maximum of £5,000.*

NEGLIGIBLE VALUE CLAIM

HMRC

.... *(insert address)*
....
....
....

.... *(insert date)*

Dear Sirs

Negligible value claim

.... ***(insert your name)***
.... ***(insert your ten digit tax reference)***

I claim relief under s.24(2) of the **Taxation of Chargeable Gains Act 1992** for the tax year ended April 5 ..... *(insert year)* in respect of my shareholding in ...... *(insert company name)* ltd/plc which cost £..... *(insert figure)*.

*[The shares are included on the "negligible value list" maintained by the Shares Valuation Office and were of negligible value as at the date of this claim].

*[The shares are not currently included on the "negligible value list" maintained by the Shares Valuation Office, but I believe the shares are of negligible value and would ask the Shares Valuation Office to consider including them on the list].

Please could you acknowledge receipt of this claim.

Yours faithfully

.... *(insert signature)*

* *delete as appropriate*

OBLIGATION FOR PAST EVENT

File note

In our opinion the Company has a present obligation for a past event. Therefore in accordance with Financial Reporting Standard 12 (FRS 12), we have decided to include a provision in the Company's accounts for the year/period ended ......*(insert date)*. We have examined the evidence available to us and are satisfied that this meets the conditions of FRS 12 as follows:

Condition 1. There is a current obligation as a result of a past event.

The past event was [e.g. wear and tear on the building caused by the Company's use of it] and the current obligation is [e.g. the new legislation /dilapidations clause in a lease etc.]. To be prudent we must presume that the Company will have to incur expenditure, as there is no evidence to suggest that it won't.

Condition 2. It is known that expenditure will be required to meet the obligation.

A list of things the Company has to do to meet the obligation has been prepared and costed. Part of the cost is self-evident from the fee quote prepared by the specialist consultant whom we intend to commission to prepare a detailed report.

Condition 3. A reliable estimate can be made of the expenditure.

The estimates of the costs involved have been prepared in consultation with the independent specialist consultant.

.... *(insert name)*
Managing/Finance Director

For and on behalf of the board of

.... *(insert name of company)*

.... *(insert date)*

PROVISION OF HOME TELEPHONE POLICY

If you are required to work from home on a regular basis, the Company will provide you with a separate telephone line for business use only.

The Company will contract directly with the telephone services provider.

You will reimburse the Company for the cost of any private calls made on a monthly basis at the actual cost (inclusive of VAT) as shown on the telephone services invoice.

Agreement

I agree to reimburse the Company for the actual cost of any private calls made using the separate business telephone line provided to me.

Signed ....

Dated ....

ROLLOVER RELIEF CLAIM

HMRC

.... *(insert address)*
....
....
. ...

.... *(insert date)*

Dear Sirs

.... ***(insert your name)***

.... ***(insert your ten digit tax reference)***

.... *(insert business name or asset description)* was sold for £ .... *(insert sale proceeds)* on .... *(insert date)*. Proceeds of £ .... *(insert amount re-invested)* were reinvested in the purchase of .... *(insert new business name or asset description)* on .... *(insert date)*. Both the asset sold and the asset acquired fall into the class of assets set out in s.155 of the **Taxation of Chargeable Gains Act 1992**.

Please accept this letter as a formal claim under s.152 of the Taxation of Chargeable Gains Act 1992 that the chargeable gain arising on the disposal is rolled over and that the base cost is reduced accordingly.

Yours faithfully

.... *(insert signature)*

SCALE RATE CLEARANCE LETTER

HMRC

.... *(insert address)*
....
....
....

.... *(insert date)*

Dear Sirs

.... ***(insert employer's PAYE reference)***

We intend to start making the following round sum payments to employees with regard to travelling and subsistence expenses:

Accommodation:

London	Per night, exclusive of meals	£75
	Per night, inclusive of meals	£96
Elsewhere	Per night, exclusive of meals	£60
	Per night, inclusive of meals	£85

Meals (when staying away overnight):		
	Breakfast	£6
	Midday meal	£7
	Evening meal	£15

We do not consider that there is any profit element in the above rates. The rates are based on an accurate survey of the costs actually concerned and are reasonable in relation to the employment involved.

Under company policy, the employee will still need to fill out an expenses claim form before a payment is made.

We should be grateful if you would confirm that we can make these round sum payments without the need for them to be taxed under PAYE.

Yours faithfully

.... *(insert signature)*

SHORT-LIFE ASSET ELECTION

HM Revenue and Customs

.... *(insert address)*

....

....

....

....

Date: .... *(insert date)*

Reference: (*insert your/your company's tax reference*)

Dear Sir

.... *(insert name of business)*

Please accept this letter as an election for short-life asset treatment in accordance with s.85 Capital Allowances Act 2001. A list of the assets for which this treatment is to apply is set out below [and continued on the attached schedule*].

Yours faithfully

....

[Director, Partner, Proprietor*]

(*delete as required)

Date asset purchased	Cost of asset	Description

SPOUSE'S JOB DESCRIPTION

1. Credit control clerk

Job title	Credit control clerk
Accountability	Accounts manager
Location	Main office (at your office address)
Brief description	To maintain and monitor 150 credit accounts
Duties and responsibilities	Cash allocation on computerised system Debt collection via telephone and standard letter Liaison with debt collection agency Some attendance at county courts Attendance of local credit meetings Maintaining credit limits Processing credit applications including credit checks Liaising with sales team
Hours of work	20 hours per week (flexible overtime may be required)
Rate of pay	£6.19 per hour (minimum)

2. PA role

Job title	Personal assistant (PA)
Accountability	Managing director (MD)
Location	Main office (at your office address)
Brief description	Work closely with the MD to provide day-to-day administrative support.
Duties and responsibilities	Screening telephone calls, enquiries and requests and handling them if they do not think it necessary to pass on to their manger Organising the MD's diary Making appointments Dealing with incoming e-mail, faxes and post

	Taking dictation Writing letters and reports Carrying out background research into subjects the manager is dealing with, and presenting findings in an easily digestible form Standing in for the MD in their absence Organising meetings Liaising with clients, suppliers and other staff Making decisions and delegating work to others when the manager is unavailable Devising and maintaining office systems to deal efficiently with paper flow, and the organisation and storage of paperwork, documents and computer-based information Taking responsibility for recruiting and training junior staff and delegating work to them Arranging travel and accommodation Travelling with the MD from time to time, to take notes at meetings, take dictation and provide general assistance in presentations
Hours of work	20 hours per week (flexible overtime may be required)
Rate of pay	£6.19 per hour (minimum)

TRADING LOSS RELIEF CLAIM

HMRC

.... *(insert address)*
....
....
....

.... *(insert date)*

Dear Sirs

.... *(insert your name)*

.... *(insert your ten digit tax reference)*

In the tax year ended April 5 ... *(insert year)*, my business made a loss of £ .... *(insert amount)*. In accordance with the provisions of s.64(2) **ITA 2007**, I elect £ .... *(insert amount)* of this loss to be offset against my other income in the tax year ended April 5 ... *(insert year)*.

In the tax year ended April 5 .... *(insert year)*, I also made capital gains (after deducting allowable losses) of £..... *(insert amount)*. In accordance with the provisions of s.71, ITA 2007, I elect for £ ..... *(insert amount)* of the trading loss to be offset against these gains.

Please could you acknowledge receipt of this claim.

Yours faithfully

.... *(insert signature)*

USING YOUR OWN CAR ON COMPANY BUSINESS POLICY

Insurance

As the driver is personally liable for any incident, you should ensure that your own private motor vehicle policy is comprehensive and permits the use of your own vehicle for the purposes of business use. The cost of acquiring this is reflected in the mileage rate.

Mileage rates

The Company will reimburse you for business mileage at the following rates:

First 10,000 miles in a tax year - 45p per mile
Over 10,000 miles - 25p per mile

Mileage claims should be made at the end of each month by completing the mileage record form and expenses claim form.

Parking fines

Parking fines and other penalties will not be reimbursed by the company.

Congestion Charge

Congestion Charges or penalties for non-payment will not be paid or reimbursed by the company.

Notes

Notes

Notes

 © 199 Tax Deductions - Everything the Taxman Doesn't Want You to Know About, Indicator FL Memo

Notes

Notes

Notes

Notes

Notes

Notes

Notes

Notes

Notes

Notes

Notes

Notes